THE RELIGION OF GOLD

Myths, Models, and the Seven Things You Need to Know to Raise Your Returns

Jeffrey Dow Jones

This work is licensed under a Creative Commons
Attribution-NonCommercial-NoDerivatives 4.0
International License.

ISBN: 1499638493
ISBN-13: 978-1499638493

For the devout gold bugs and the heathen haters,
the atheists and agnostics, too.

Contents

The Box   11
Introduction   15

Part 1 — A Brief History of Gold 21

Chapter 1.   Ancient History 25
Chapter 2.   Middle History 32
Chapter 3.   Modern History 37

Part 2 — A New Framework of Belief 41

Chapter 4.   Drivers & Data Sets 46
Chapter 5.   Serendipitous Happenstance or Cold Calculation? 51
Chapter 6.   It's My Gold and I'll Value It How I Please 58
Chapter 7.   Putting the Free Market to the Test 64
Chapter 8.   A Re-Writing of Gold's History 69
Chapter 9.   Caveats Aplenty 76

Part 3 — A Basic Projection Model 85

Chapter 10. Estimating Future Returns 87

Part 4 — The Seven Things Every Investor Needs to Know About Gold 97

Chapter 11. Gold Doesn't Do Anything 100
Chapter 12. It's Not the Inflation Hedge You Think It Is 104
Chapter 13. Gold Isn't Money 113
Chapter 14. Gold Is Not A Safe Haven 120

Chapter 15.	Cash Has Been a Better Investment............127
Chapter 16.	We're Never Going Back to a Gold Standard. 136
Chapter 17.	Every Investor Should Own Gold.................144
Conclusion	152

Appendix: Alternative Gold Strategies . 157

Building a Practical, Simple Strategy for Gold 158

    "4-Bucket" Strategy..160

    "10-Bucket" Strategy 164

    Basic Trend Following Strategy 168

    Lazy Trend Following Strategy 170

    Trend + Signal Strategy (Leveraged)................ 175

About the Author 179

Acknowledgements 181

In the years after the California gold rush, the philosopher John Ruskin would tell a colorful story:

Once there was a rich man who boarded a ship, carrying all of his wealth in gold coins. At sea, the ship encountered a violent storm and began to capsize. The man, frantic about being forced to abandon ship, strapped all two hundred pounds of gold to a belt about his waist and leapt overboard, promptly sinking straight to the ocean floor.

At this point in the story, Ruskin would smile and ask, "Now, as he was sinking – had *he* the gold?"

"Or had the gold *him*?"

The Box

The Box

I'll never forget my own first experience with gold. It's not as colorful as John Ruskin's tale, but it's one that was incredibly influential, establishing the initial foundation upon which all of my interactions with gold from that point have been based.

You see, I am the son of a gold bug. My dad was one of those guys for whom gold truly *was* religion. He was too pragmatic to leap off a sinking ship with a hundred pounds of gold strapped to his belt. But he was one of those guys whom gold *had*. He was an ardent believer in gold and what it represented in both a fiscal-monetary and metaphorical-spiritual sense. Born in 1930 and a child of the Great Depression and War, it's possible that these beliefs were unavoidably woven into his DNA.

Before founding an investment firm and launching his own fund, he was a local coin dealer. I'm sure that was a great business in the late 70's when gold was going up, but I understand now why he gave it up in the early 80's and pursued a different line of work. I doubt people were buying much gold as the bubble was deflating.

Despite that, he was a man with an undying love of precious metals. He wrote a newsletter about gold. He kept bags of silver in a vault downtown. He was an oddball that buried bags of pure-copper pennies in the backyard. I was lectured repeatedly as a youth to someday dig them up when the metallurgic value of the copper in each penny was higher than the $0.01 face value. My brother and I were given an honest-to-God treasure map for their location[1].

One day when I was eight or nine years old, he came home and set a small box — maybe half the size of a shoe box — down on the kitchen counter. I picked it up. It was very heavy. Inside was a dozen or so plastic cylinders. They were sealed tightly and he would not permit me to open any of them. He did uncork one tube, however, and emptied out a single, radiant coin.

"Daddy," I said. "What's that?"

"It's your college education."

There were probably two or three hundred one-ounce Canadian Gold Maple Leafs in the box.

It might have been $100,000 of gold sitting right there on the kitchen counter. Or more. Later that night I would eat my Kraft mac 'n cheese on that same hallowed ground. That counter was where we played Chinese Checkers. Now it was a holy spot.

As I reflect on the memory, I wonder how much of his *entire* net worth was sitting there in front of us in that moment. My little mind couldn't fathom that at the time, of course. The enormity of it left an impression nonetheless.

Who knows why we recall the specific experiences that we do from childhood. Certain moments leave an impact while others are forgotten. Some of these events can seem rather arbitrary.

---

[1] After my mom moved out of that old house years ago, we finally dug up the bags of copper pennies. Unfortunately, my dad's engineering execution wasn't as good as his market foresight. The burlap bags had completely disintegrated. It's possible he wasn t intending the thesis to take two decades to play out!

Whatever the reason, seeing that box of gold on the kitchen counter would impact me in profound ways through the rest of my life.

As a boy, I remember being utterly transfixed by those coins, if not on the surface then subconsciously so. I wonder if there's something deeper that attracts us to gold, something woven into our genetic code, imprinted by God, or baked into the marrow of our bones. A favorite anecdote of mine and one you can try at home is to produce a gold coin at a cocktail party and toss it around. Watch how everyone's expressions regard it. It is equal parts awe and lust.

I think this might be why the history of the gold market is one of madness. Gold is a corollary to our own maddening history as humans. We and it are intimately and unavoidably entwined. That knowledge and that feeling follows me everywhere. It haunts me to this day.

By the time I went to college, those coins were worth half of what he paid. He always hoped I'd go to Stanford but I wound up at UCLA. So at least tuition was cheaper than what he originally budgeted! I don't know what happened to that box and if it actually wound up actually paying for my four years at school. When I graduated, I thought of those coins. I dream of them regularly. I can still see that box.

After graduation my first job was as a commodities broker. Gold at that point was trading in the mid-$200's. It had gone down for almost twenty straight years and was sitting at a generational low. Every single person I talked to about gold hated it. Everyone. It was taboo and no rational gentleman would consider it a worthwhile investment. Even many of the hardline gold bugs had given up the ghost.

If there's one thing we should always be mindful of with gold, it's how dramatically sentiment can change – not just day to day, but decade to decade.

Despite those ever-changing winds of sentiment, Ruskin's tale of the man leaping overboard with a belt full of gold will always captivate us. Gold will dazzle even if we believe its prospects to be poor. This means that any future outcome is in play.

We should be surprised by nothing.

Today as I reflect on that box, I realize what my father was really doing was making an investment in me. That box may not have literally been for my college education, but it was something large and weighty sitting on the counter nonetheless. Intended or not, it put the hopes and expectations for me into perspective.

Who knows how much that gold would be worth today. Certainly a great deal. He invested a lot of money in me and there's not a day that goes by when I don't wonder if that investment was worth it.

I can only speculate.

And keep faith.

Introduction

The book you now hold in your hands had an eerie and auspicious birth.

In late 2010, my coworkers finally got sick of listening to me run around the office every day and rant about how expensive gold was. Our firm was an NFA & CFTC registered commodity trading advisor and commodity pool operator, so it wasn't like a discussion about gold was totally out of place. They were tired of hearing it every single day, though, and whether I had sufficiently convinced them or not, they started hinting that I ought to direct my gold rants elsewhere. Politely at first. Later, bluntly.

I sought a broader platform.

It began with a prediction on one of our websites, a weekly blog I wrote on various market topics. As part of our "Predictions for 2011" newsletter[2], I stated that gold was in a bubble.

> *I'm feeling increasingly confident that we're in a gold bubble right now. I have no idea how far into this bubble we are and I*

---

[2] Alpine Advisor, *Predictions for 2011*, http://cornicecapital.com/AlpineAdvisor/2011/01/06/predictions-for-2011-part-one/ (January 6, 2011)

> have no idea how far this bubble will go. I am neither smart enough nor stupid enough to predict when or why it'll end.
>
> Gold is 100% speculation right now. By buying gold, you are speculating that:
>
> 1. the bubble will continue
> 2. or heavy duty inflation will materialize before too much longer
>
> ...If Gold does get to $2,000/oz — and I think it's even-odds that happens in the next year or three — you need to understand that you are playing with fire.

Unlike most Wall Street analysts, I've never been one to take predictions very seriously. Not others', and certainly not my own. Predicting the future is impossible and believing that there are people in the market who can is one of the biggest mistakes that amateur investors make. In any case, the annual ritual of looking ahead over the course of the year and speculating about how it may unfold is one of the most enjoyable and entertaining exercises that I engage in. It's the fact that I don't take any of it very seriously that allows me to have fun.

But apparently, that wasn't enough. Simply getting on public record about gold being in a bubble didn't stop the daily office rants. For some reason, I could not shut up about gold. It was as though some evil spirit has possessed me. My only hope was to exorcise the demon.

I sought the help of a priest and a bigger podium.

In February of 2011, I published an article at *Seeking Alpha*, a popular financial website for research and market commentary.

The article was about gold being in the midst of the speculative bubble. My research was shaky, my charts and models were flawed. Like any version 1.0 product, there were bugs aplenty. This was only the beginning, however, and what I set out to do in that article would ultimately become the foundation for the book now in your hands.

At the time, the idea that gold might be in or headed for some type of bubble was so controversial, the site's editors awkwardly changed the headline of the piece even though the opening paragraphs directly contradicted the title text. It's an amusing relic still stored in one of the forgotten corners of the Internet.

Jeffrey Dow Jones, Alpine Advisor (343 clicks)
Hedge fund analyst, newsletter provider, research analyst, portfolio strategy
Profile | Send Message | ✓ Following (1,869)   Edit Article

Gold May Not Be a Bubble, But It's Also Not a Good Hedge Against Inflation

Feb. 14, 2011 12:08 PM ET | 50 comments | About: **GLD**
Disclosure: I have no positions in any stocks mentioned, and no plans to initiate any positions within the next 72 hours

One of our predictions for 2011 was that gold was in a bubble. After stirring the peak oil pot here on Seeking Alpha, I'm not sure I want to kick another hornet's next.

But, whatever: **gold is in a bubble right now**.

I can hear all you gold bulls getting ready to fire off an angry e-mail right now, but hold on a second before you do.

The article received 2,132 pageviews, laughable for a site with over 2 million unique monthly visitors. I published another article on dividend stocks that exact same day and it received over 35,000 pageviews.

In 2011, gold was as popular as it had been in nearly thirty years. Enthusiasm was riding high. The public had little appetite for pessimistic arguments that pushed the other direction. Really, who could blame them?

My coworkers enjoyed the article, though. They encouraged me to expand on the argument. And with the demon inside me still un-exorcised, that spring, I began writing a book.

I gave it up that summer, though.

Gold would surge to nearly $2,000/oz.

I was as wrong as could be. I threw my arms up in frustration and admitted defeat. I buried that "Book - Gold Bubble" Word doc in a forgotten archive deep in the bowels of Windows Explorer, alongside other aborted projects, failed research, and bizarre, semi-coherent rumblings.

I shut up about gold for a while.

My coworkers didn't miss the distraction and seemed happy to get back to work.

Three years later, with the benefit of hindsight, we can now recognize that the move to $2,000/oz did represent the peak of a speculative bubble. The deflation of that bubble shortly thereafter was clear, if uneven. It didn't finally "pop" until 2013.

That popping got the spirits stirring again. I dug the old spreadsheets and Word files out of the archive and dusted them off. I updated all the data, patched all the holes, and started sharpening the blade, ready to wield the argument in battle. Hopefully more skillfully than I'd done in the spring of 2011.

One of the factors that help improve the argument was continual, ferocious opposition to the idea that gold might be far more expensive than its fundamentals suggested. In order to make such a claim, I needed not just excellent data and a logical thesis, I needed an eloquent and convincing delivery.

This book, warts and all, represents the latest version of this argument. It also includes an entertaining history of gold for the layman, as well as a list of some of the most-important and least-appreciated characteristics of gold.

Some will be convinced, others less so. But as I learned back in 2011, it really doesn't matter. None of us know what the future has in store. We fight about this and we fight about that. We thrust our attacks and parry in defense. Occasionally, it's unclear who it even is that we're fighting or what started our crusade in the first place.

The reality, however, is that we're all on the same side. We direct our arguments at each other, but our common enemy is *uncertainty*. Anything that casts light on the shadows of the unknown is worthwhile. It should be celebrated by all.

I'm excited to finally be publishing this book. It wouldn't be possible without the help of my coworkers and family.

Today, the evil spirits have finally released their grip on my soul. The exorcism worked. And what finally did it wasn't all the ranting and writing and researching and coming up coherent thesis and body of evidence to support it. It was the realization I had it all wrong from the start:

Neither you nor I have any clue what lurks in the years ahead. Instead of fighting over certainties, let's use this as a trailhead for discovery. Let's see what else we can learn.

About gold and about each other.

Introduction

Part I

A Brief History of Gold

The history of gold is rich and complex, complete with action and drama worthy of any work of fiction. Our complex affair with gold has persisted for thousands of years and it will surely outlive each and every one of us. A thousand years from now gold will glitter in the eyes and hearts of humanity and it will do the same a thousand years after that. It will hypnotize us as it always has. It will kindle our souls.

This is not intended to be a history text. However, a quick romp through the history of gold is a good way to get an appreciation for exactly what we're dealing with. Like any naturally occurring resource, gold has been around for all time. But it wasn't until early societies started to organize themselves that the true tale of gold began to unfold.

Unlike elements such as iron, uranium, or crude oil which didn't really get interesting until humans figured out to use them for a specific purpose, gold was important from day one. Gold was a way to measure, store, and communicate *wealth*, a concept that pre-dates any industry and will outlast any functional or elemental use. Eons from now when we're travelling the galaxy in rocket ships, we may not have much need for aluminum or natural gas. But gold will still be important. We'll still want it.

Gold has an intrinsic appeal that everything else found in the earth's crust lacks. To borrow from Keats, *this is all we know about gold, and all we need to know*.

Intrinsic value is the most important factor in any analysis one conducts. Later, in parts two and three we'll investigate different ways to think about and measure intrinsic value.

Chapter 1.

ANCIENT HISTORY

By most accounts, the ancient Sumerians, a society of relatively advanced agrarians in early Mesopotamia, were among the first humans in history to use gold[3]. The earliest record of Sumer dates back to around 5000-6000 BCE but it wasn't until somewhere around 3000 BCE that they began fashioning the soft, shiny metal into jewelry. This coincided with their flourishing economy and culture. Little is known about the original inhabitants of what is today Eastern Europe, but discoveries in the region suggest an early society in the Transylvanian Alps using gold perhaps a thousand years earlier than the Sumerians.

Of all the major ancient cultures, none are more strongly identified with gold than the ancient Egyptians. The Egyptians considered gold a divine metal because it shined brilliantly like the sun. To them it was literally the

---

[3] National Mining Association. *The History of Gold* Washington DC, USA. http://www.nma.org/pdf/gold/gold_history.pdf

"skin of the gods" and it was used extensively to adorn statues of their gods. Only kings, whose power descended from the Sun God himself, were allowed to wear gold as jewelry. Gold was buried in their tombs and taken with them into the afterlife[4]. In the tomb of Djer, a first-dynasty king who ruled three thousand years before the birth of Christ, archaeologists found a mummified arm laden with gold jewelry. It is one of the earliest-dated gold discoveries of significance.

Egyptian culture was associated with gold because Egypt was full of it. The Nubian region in Northeastern Africa along the Nile River produced huge quantities of gold. It was one of the central reasons for ancient Egypt's fantastic economic success. By 1500 BCE the Egyptians had accumulated tremendous wealth and were exporting significant amounts of gold to surround societies. It was an era of unprecedented prosperity[5].

Ramesses the Great ascended to the throne around 1280 BCE and he proceeded to build more temples and statues than any pharaoh to date. As it occurs in nature, gold is a very soft, non-durable metal. But by this point the Egyptians had mastered the techniques of pounding gold into leaf and alloying it with other metals to enhance its durability and utility. This was one of the most significant periods of advancement in history for jewelry making, many techniques which are still in use today. Egyptian craftsman were so skilled that many artifacts from this era

---

[4] Jimmy Dunn, "Golden Egypt",
http://www.touregypt.net/featurestories/gold.htm; Last viewed on 16/06/2014
[5] National Mining Association. The History of Gold Washington DC, USA.
http://www.nma.org/pdf/gold/gold_history.pdf

still exist today. These metallurgical advancements also helped lay the foundation for a relatively new concept: currency.

FIGURE 1.1 GOLD PLATED SARCOPHAGUS

Elsewhere in the Middle East around 1500 BCE the first gold coins were minted[6]. The famous Shekel was

---

[6] National Mining Association. *The History of Gold* Washington DC, USA. http://www.nma.org/pdf/gold/gold_history.pdf

born. It was the first time in recorded history that gold was officially used as a medium of exchange. The Shekel was originally made from electrum, a pale-yellow, naturally occurring alloy consisting of gold and silver. This made it much more durable and practical to use in the daily exchange for goods and services.

A few centuries later the Chinese would also begin using gold coins as a form of money. In ancient China, the minting of coins from a variety of metals – copper, iron, lead, silver, and gold – was widespread. Gold and silver ingots were quite popular and in 1091 BC, little squares of solid gold were legalized as money[7]. Our association of gold with wealth and currency began to take on a new, more formal dimension, one that still exists today. Three thousand years later, the idea of gold as money and a store of value is impossible to separate from the metal itself.

As cultures matured and early societies advanced, the history of gold became progressively more dramatic. Croesus, a fifth-century BCE king in what is today Turkey, is credited with using the first *pure* gold coins. After he was defeated and captured by the Persians, Croesus' gold was immediately adopted for use for their coins[8]. Praised by Herodotus for his wealth, the phrase "rich as Croesus" carries as much majesty and magnificence today as it did in ancient times.

In 334 BCE Alexander the Great made his legendary crossing of the Hellespont with over 40,000 soldiers. It was one of the greatest military campaigns in recorded history. Two short years later Alexander had conquered

---

[7] Chinese Ancient Currency, http://www.chinahighlights.com/travelguide/culture/chinese-ancient-currency.htm.

[8] Gold Coins – A Brief History, http://taxfreegold.co.uk/goldcoinsbriefhistory.html

The Religion of Gold

all of Egypt. His prize? Untold quantities of gold. The wealth of his empire expanded tremendously with this victory.

It is here that widespread fascination with and hunger for gold evolved in a magical new direction. The Greeks of ancient Alexandria began dabbling with alchemy, the art of turning ordinary metal into precious gold. This was believed to be possible by way of the philosopher's stone (sorcerer's stone), a mysterious and possibly-primordial substance capable not only of transmuting lead into gold, but also rejuvenation and achieving immortality. The Greek king, Midas, is in a way a mythological manifestation of this idea.

The most famous and well-documented era of gold coin use was in ancient Rome. When the Romans conquered Spain during the Punic wars, they gained access to a highly productive gold mining region. Later, after Julius Caesar conquered Gaul, he brought back enough gold to fund his entire army and pay off all of Rome's debts. This influx of wealth stabilized the economy and laid the foundation for a new era of prosperity under Caesar Augustus.

Figure 1.2 Silver Denarius

The silver *denarius* is what typically comes to mind when one thinks of ancient Roman coins. They were commonly used in the transactions of the time and many of these coins still exist today. The gold *aureus*, however, was the most desired. These gold and silver coins would be used as the standard medium of exchange in the Roman Empire for the next 500 years. It was one of the foundations of their long success.

After his conquest, Julius Caesar standardized the value of these coins by fixing the amount of gold and silver they were minted with. But by the reign of Nero, Rome had run into problems once again. With their backs against the monetary wall, the emperor devalued the currency by decreasing the amount of gold the coins were minted with[9]. This is perhaps the earliest and most famous example of price inflation and currency debasement. Its example is cited frequently today, particular by those for whom inflation is their chief financial nightmare.

Inflation played a significant role in the decline of the Roman Empire. By 300-400 CE the budget to support all the roads, aqueducts, and armies was too onerous. Tax increases couldn't keep up and by debasing the currency, despite the originally good intentions of backing it with precious metals, stoked hyperinflation. This fiscal collapse pushed the Roman Empire towards its ultimate failure, accelerating collapses in its government, economy, and culture[10].

This event, chronicled with accuracy and color by Edward Gibbon in *The History of the Decline and Fall of the Roman Empire*, would stage the backdrop for gold and frame our complicated emotional relationship with it for the next fifteen-hundred years.

---

[9] Micheal Valdivivielso, *The Fall of the Roman Empire* http://www.roman-empire.net/articles/article-003.html;
[10] Ibid.

Chapter 2.

MIDDLE HISTORY

Neither gold nor its emerging utility as a store of value disappeared with the ancient Romans. Somewhere between 742 and 814, Charlemagne conquered the Huns[11], a pagan Asian horde that inhabited what is today Hungary. He plundered vast quantities of gold, leveraging this newfound wealth to direct his campaign westward and take control over much of Western Europe.

During that era, one of the largest sources of gold was in West Africa, and the commercial and sea power of Italian cities enabled them to compete for access to the North African outlets of this trade. By 1252 enough gold was passing into the cities of Florence and Genoa for them to launch gold coinages.

The great Republic of Venice would use gold coins as well. In 1284, near the height of their power, the Venetian gold Ducat, famed for its purity and accepted in

---

[11] Fine, John Van Antwerp (1991). *The early medieval Balkans: a critical survey from the sixth to the late twelfth century.* University of Michigan Press. p. 78.

international trade[12]. It was the most popular coin in the world and would remain so for the next five centuries until the Venetian empire weakened amidst an epoch of protest before finally falling to the armies of Napoleon. For that, the French would win 3 million francs in gold.

FIGURE 1.3 THE VENETIAN DUCAT

Britain would also begin minting its own gold coins. With the Norman conquest, a metallic currency standard was re-established and by the 13th century the entire monetary system was based on gold and silver. The pound

---

[12] Numismaster, *The History of Gold Coins* http://www.numismaster.com/ta/inside_numis.jsp?page=history-gold-coins

Sterling was once, literally, derived from a pound of Sterling silver[13]. In 1284, Great Britain would issue its first widely-accepted gold coin, the Florin, and by 1377 its monetary system was based strictly on gold & silver.

The early and middle history of gold is centered in Europe because that's where the best records were being kept. But in 1275 CE, Marco Polo wrote about the Far East, a land where he claimed the gold riches were vast beyond belief. A similar history was unfolding in East Asia too.

Jade had historically been the main symbol of wealth and status in ancient Chinese culture. Archaeologists have unearthed gold and silver ingots from ancient China, but there's virtually no documented use of gold in the centuries after the Han Dynasty (220 CE)[14]. But by the time of Marco Polo's travels, that had changed. Gold had adopted many of jade's qualities as a symbol of wealth. China was also in the process of slowly adopting a silver-backed currency standard and by the end of the Ming Dynasty in 1644, silver coins would be widely circulated[15].

In the early 1500's, King Ferdinand II of Aragon began launching expeditions to the newly discovered lands in the Western Hemisphere. It was in 1511 that King Ferdinand, architect of the Spanish Inquisition, also uttered those chilling, immortal words:

> *Get gold – humanely if possible – but by all hazards, get gold.*

---

[13] Blanchard, Ian, *Mining, Metallurgy and Minting in the Middle Ages*, Vol. 3; 2005

[14] TED Case Studies; 'Jade and its Historic and Modern Meanings for Trade'; http://www1.american.edu/ted/jade.htm

[15] Ibid.

FIGURE 1.4 KING FERDINAND II OF ARAGON

Motives aside, Ferdinand was pointed in the right direction in terms of gold. Through the next two centuries, Spanish conquistadors extracted massive quantities of gold from the New World. It was an efficient machine. The conquistadors would trade for it or simply take it while their ace *flotas* sailed it safely home, even amidst storms, pirates, and two decades of harassment from Sir Francis Drake, the "master-thief of the unknown world." While on its voyage to circumnavigate the world, Drake and his famous galleon, the *Golden Hind,* nabbed six tons of treasure from the Spanish *Nuestra*, one of the largest plunders in history. In current dollars, it was well over $200 million in treasure. A constant thorn in the Spanish Armada's side, King Philip II was rumored to have offered 20,000 ducats for *El Draque's* head.

Despite this explosion in wealth, Spain proved unable to build anything that would endure. They weren't the first empire to squander huge amounts of mineral wealth. Nor would they be the last. Like the ancient Romans and many other nations in history, Spain spent money more quickly than it came in, frittering it away on unnecessary luxuries, an overextended naval armada, and endlessly-mounting debt obligations.

Ferdinand's dreams were never fully realized, but the New World proved the place to be. In 1700 gold was discovered in the Portuguese colony of Brazil. A few decades later Brazil would become the largest supplier of gold in the world, accounting for a staggering two thirds of total global output[16].

By the Renaissance, many of the world's major economies had shifted away from using gold as currency, using other types of coins instead. It was in 1717 that Isaac Newtown, master of the Royal Mint, famously affixed the price of gold in Great Britain to 84 shillings per ounce. The coins may not have been gold, but the standard was.

That price would hold for the next two hundred years.

---

[16] National Mining Association. The History of Gold Washington DC, USA.
http://www.nma.org/pdf/gold/gold_history.pdf

Chapter 3.
MODERN HISTORY

Elsewhere in the New World, other interesting things were afoot.
During and briefly after the Revolutionary War, all the gold in the newly formed United States of America still came from England. In 1787 the U.S. minted its first gold coin, the Brasher Doubloon. It was a private coin but by the next decade the Coinage Act established the Mint and put the United States officially on its own gold standard. The U.S. Dollar was defined at that point to be equal to 24.75 grains of gold. After a few complicated conversions, it worked out to $19.39 per ounce.

One of the most colorful phases of gold's history – at least for Americans – was the gold rush of the 19th century. If nothing else, this period of U.S. history is particularly illustrative of the gripping psychology that has always existed around gold – from the ancient Egyptians to the Roman Empire to Ferdinand and Isabella's conquistadors.

The first documented gold discovery in the United States was in 1799. A 17 pound gold nugget – worth several hundred thousand dollars at today's prices – was found in North Carolina. Immediately after that our first flirtations with gold fever began.

One of the most famous events in the American history of gold occurred in 1848. That was when James W. Marshall, a carpenter who had been hired by John Sutter to build a sawmill, discovered a few flecks of gold in the American River in Central California. His discovery triggered the gold rush and catalyzed the westward expansion and development of the United States. In twenty short years, the U.S. would have a transcontinental railroad that opened the door for a new era of economic expansion. As the final spike was driven, the newfound resources of the West moved meaningfully closer to the capital markets of the East.

A lesser-known, but arguably more important gold discovery happened in 1886. George Harrison, an Australian gold miner, discovered gold while digging up stones to build a house in the Witwatersrand area of South Africa. Few in the West have heard of this, but since then, that region has been the source of roughly 40% of all the gold ever mined from the ground. Today it contains approximately half of the world's proven gold reserves and it's also home of two of the deepest mines on earth, each of which extends 12,000 feet below the earth's surface.

In 1896, gold was discovered in the Klondike region of the Yukon in north-western Canada. This was the final phase of gold fever, and what is commonly misunderstood about the Klondike gold rush is that was functionally over once it began in earnest. By the time news had reached Seattle and San Francisco, and eager prospectors finally arrived in the cold North, most of the opportunities had been claimed. Of the 100,000+ gold-seekers who set out for the Klondike, only a third would make it all the way, and only a fraction of those would ever strike gold.

Such is the cruel nature of a "gold rush," a term that today applies to far more than just gold.

FIGURE 1.5 THE KONDIKE GOLD RUSH. MINERS ASCENDING THE CHILKOOT PASS.

The excitement and ultimate disappointment of the Klondike wasn't the last event that shaped Americans' complicated psychology of gold. The 20th century would contain equal amounts of drama, though this would unfold within the confines of Washington D.C. rather of the previously-wild and now-tapped West.

Modern History

Part 2

A New Framework of Belief

Drivers & Data Sets

The Religion of Gold

The story of gold is every bit as rich as its color. In many ways, nothing in human history is like it. But gold, its history, and the culture surrounding it bear an odd resemblance to something rather unexpected: religion.

This is especially true when we use the most literal definition for the term "religion." Gold indeed has its own rather well-organized structure of beliefs, rituals, and causes. These views are quite popular in certain circles and clung to with ardor and intense faith. As an example, one view that is central to the religion of gold is a distrust of paper currencies. Fiat currencies are backed only by a promise from the government, i.e., they have value because the government says they have value. There is certainly no shortage of examples throughout history where these promises have been broken and individuals who had wealth stored in paper currencies have been left shivering in the cold. Gold, as an asset that has successfully stored value for millennia, can represent an attractive alternative to relying on that promise. Only through gold can individuals achieve monetary salvation.

Consider a more metaphorical interpretation of gold as religion. Gold has been an important building block and economic pillar in nearly all the great societies in history. Just as many of the most powerful cultures were rich with religion, the most powerful economies all utilized gold in one way or another. There exist robust evidence to justify one's faith in gold.

Gold has been evangelized, literally worshipped, sung in gospels, and has motivated people and societies to do incredible – and occasionally bizarre – things. What else could compel us to endure the harsh cold of the Klondike or send 48,000 troops into Asia Minor?

In a modern sense, gold and religion are commonly conflated because the gold market and its investors tend to be highly dogmatic. When it comes to gold, investors tend to either believe or not believe. The religion of gold is true or not true. There is no mind changing.

As any good scientist, historian, or investor must, we have to separate our personal feelings and biases from what we're analyzing. Really, when we study gold, we must study it the way any religious scholar would. We must leave our emotion at the door and focus on the facts. We must make no moral judgments and simply look to connect the dots between cause and effect, phenomenon and belief. We must study the data for what it is rather than what we want it to be, or what it needs to be to justify the pillars of our faith.

We have to separate anecdotal legend from truth.

The good news is that as we move into the 20th century, our analysis shifts. The colorful anecdotes recede, replaced by an array of informative and reliable data sets as well as a new, driving question: "how much is this stuff worth?"

With that question as our compass, we can establish a baseline for understanding its price.

During the 20th century, there is one economic history that matters above all others: that of the United States.

Finally able to leverage the geopolitical advantage of being the first and only developed nation in history to have coasts on both of the planet's major oceans as well as an efficient internal network connecting them, the U.S.

would embark on an unprecedented growth trajectory and enjoy a massive advantage in terms of global trade. A surge in population growth during the middle of the century and playing key role in Europe's post-War reconstruction would solidify the United States' role as the dominant global economy. By extension, its policy and practices with respect to gold would in many ways become the only one that mattered.

It is to the U.S. that we now turn and where our history of gold begins to change shape. It's also where we can finally start asking important questions about gold, such as what factors influence its price, and ultimately, what it ought to be worth. We do away with cultural tradition and teachings of faith and instead begin to look closely at economic data.

Chapter 4.

DRIVERS & DATA SETS

We all know and agree that when it comes to the stock market, very long-term returns are a function of a few simple factors:
- GDP growth & corporate earnings.
- Dividends.
- Inflation.
- An element of psychology (i.e. price multiple expansion & contraction)

That's pretty much it. All the action in the stock market over the last century can be explained by with those four variables. You won't encounter anybody in the financial industry who disagrees with that.

The reason why we spend time studying these variables is because if we know *exactly* what these variables will look like, then we can predict the stock market's long-term return with accuracy. In other words: we can make a lot of money.

One of the reasons why it's so difficult to make a lot of money in the stock market is because it's tricky to get a handle on those variables. Dividends and inflation are easy enough to forecast, but GDP and corporate earnings can fluctuate a lot. New economic cycles can strike without warning.

Gross Domestic Product (GDP) in the United States has grown at a fairly consistent rate over the last century but that rate has varied depending on the economic cycle. During the post-War years, it averaged over 7%. During the last decade it has averaged under 3%. We can guess about what future economic growth will look like, but we can't predict when crises or recessions will strike. Nor can we predict how much they'll throw the economy off trend.

There are macro variables that impact the long-term trends in the markets as well. During the era of globalization, old winners and losers have been reshuffled. Different countries are economically important today, as are these nations' different industries and companies. These variables can throw off trends previously believed to be reliable.

Psychology is also a wild card. Investor sentiment can carry prices to unimaginable highs the way we saw during the tech bubble. It can also depress valuations to unimaginable lows such as we saw in early 2009 after the financial crisis. Fortunately, psychology tends to even out over the long run. When it moves too far in one direction and prices reach a level where they are too difficult to justify with the underlying fundamentals, psychology begins to swing back the other way.

The good news is that with gold, building a long-term model to explain the price is much easier than with stocks. As a real asset, gold is driven primarily by just one variable: inflation. More specifically, the value of gold depends on the value of the dollars in which it is denominated. We're in luck because we have a terrific long-term data set on this, the Consumer Price Index.

Some analysts don't like the CPI. They claim it understates the true rate of inflation. They criticize it because its calculation methodology changes over time. These objections are understandable, as the CPI, like any index or indicator is imperfect.

In truth, calculating a systemic price level is a terrifyingly difficult task. The nature of the economy and what we buy and sell is quite different today than it was a hundred years ago. We spend a different percentage of our incomes on very different things. On top of that, how do we account for improvements in quality and function over the ears? I have a device in my pocket that enables me to communicate with virtually any individual on the planet and gives me access to nearly all the knowledge that mankind possesses. On it, I can watch nearly any movie ever made or listen to any song ever recorded. This device would be unfathomably expensive a few decades ago. A century ago, such a thing would be disregarded as fantasy. But it only cost me a few hundred dollars. How should these types of factors affect how we broadly measure all prices in the system?

The bigger problem is that, so far, no one in the world has come up with a *better* way of tracking inflation. At least not one that extends far enough into the past. Warts aside, the CPI is as good as it gets. The really intelligent people at the Bureau of Labor Statistics do the best they can to determine the true rate of inflation in the U.S. economy, and to their credit, they do an excellent job. Inflation has become an especially popular and occasionally-touchy topic in recent years, and the CPI has some competition now.

One of the more interesting new metrics is MIT's "Billion Prices Project". They monitor price the daily price fluctuations of over 5 million retail products from 300 online retailers in 70 countries. As it happens, their results are remarkably similar to the CPI.

FIGURE 2.1 CONSUMER PRICE INDEX VS. BILLION PRICES PROJECT
SOURCE: STATE STREET

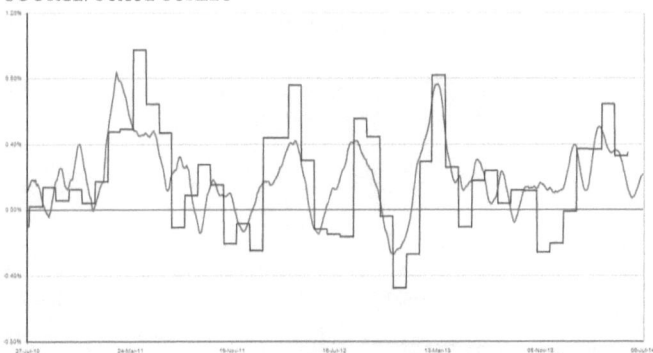

For some investors, this data set is much more useful as it gets calculated every day. The CPI takes more time to calculate and it lags a bit. Inflationary spikes will appear more quickly in the Billion Prices Project than in the CPI.

For the purposes of our work, the CPI will suffice. All we're seeking to establish is a basic, long-term, fundamental trend line for gold. As inflation rises, so does the price of gold. At least over the long run. This is accepted as gospel in both the gold community and the community of paper currency enthusiasts. The data support this belief as well.

Before we move on, there is a slim possibility that you don´t believe gold is or should be influenced by the rate of inflation and the way inflation affects the value of the Dollars in which gold is denominated. You may believe that other factors influence the price of gold – and over the short-run, psychology is certainly one of these.

This belief in the power of separate price drivers for gold is understandable. But let me tell you a quick story. It involves black magic and high priests and government conspiracies.

It might just change your mind.

Chapter 5.

Serendipitous Happenstance or Cold Calculation?

Our history of gold resumes in the year 1900, shortly after the gold rushes in California and Alaska. By this point, "gold fever" was dying down. Thanks to the influx of supply, the United States' gold reserves were flush. The government was hard at work at laying an economic and monetary foundation that would be sounder than dismal, deflationary years following the Civil War.

1900 is a less arbitrary beginning for this chapter than you'd think. It wasn't just the first year of a new century and an easy entry point for calendar math. (Working with dates in Excel prior to 1900 is a huge hassle I have a secret theory that that's why you see so few charts go back before then. Analysts are a lazy lot.)

1900 was the year when the Gold Standard Act was passed.

Serendipitous Happenstance or Cold Calculation?

FIGURE 2.2 PRESIDENT WILLIAM MCKINLEY
source: Wikimedia Commons

Unlike most of today's legislation, this one actually did what the title suggests. President William McKinley signed the bill into law and, presto, the United States was on a gold standard. One dollar was fixed to "25 8/10 grains of gold at 90% purity." By extension, one ounce of gold was assigned a dollar value of $20.67.

The price, which had informally stood for seventy years, would stand under law for another three decades.

The level of inflation, however, would not stand still for three decades. It would explode during World War I and then turn into a different sort of nightmare, systemic *de*flation, during the early years of the Great Depression. Under the specter of deflation, the idea of sustainable economic recovery seemed impossible.

By 1934, something had to be done and the wizards of the Roosevelt administration were just the people to do it. So Congress passed the Gold Reserve Act of 1934. That was when it became illegal for the public to own gold. Citizens were forced to sell all their gold to the Treasury.

We occasionally forget that gold's anecdotal history is one of utterly-unpredictable drama. Today, the idea of being forced to sell one's gold to the government sounds completely absurd. It's hard for investors today to comprehend such a thing. But this event actually happened. The U.S. government actually did confiscate all the public gold. In the grand scheme of gold's thousand year history, it wasn't even that long ago.

Events like this are an obvious lesson that anything is possible when it comes to gold. But more generally, this is a gentle reminder that we should always practice caution when performing apples-to-apples comparisons of today's economic data to the data of yesteryear. Environments can change. Sometimes, dramatically. The raw numbers don't always tell that part of the story. History is a slippery, ever-changing thing, and it can be dangerous to only view the past through the prism of today.

For our purposes, the most important piece of this historic legislation was the price. The nominal price of gold was reset from $20.67/oz to $35/oz. That was a 40% devaluation of the Dollar under the terms of the gold standard terms. The U.S. Treasury saw the value of their gold holdings increase by a tidy $50 billion overnight (in current dollar terms).

Serendipitous Happenstance or Cold Calculation?

The good news is that the move worked. The country realized that these guys weren't messing around. And the economy got back on track. By the end of 1934, the economy was growing at a 17% clip. GDP would continue to expand at a double digit rate through the end of 1937.

Revaluing gold and devaluing the Dollar was also successful at slaying the deflation dragon. After deflation of around -10% per year, the CPI turned around and started expanding again. Obviously, there were a lot of factors that helped reverse the country from these ugly trends -- this is what former Fed Chair Ben Bernanke is an expert on, the basis of which sets the philosophical tone for today's global monetary policy. But the key point is that after this historic intervention, the price level started going up again.

This is when our first magical coincidence occurs.

Had the Gold Standard Act of 1900 never been passed and had the price of gold simply been allowed to rise and fall in accordance with the rate of inflation, the gold price would have landed on January 1, 1934 at $34.57.

In other words, after the re-setting of the gold price in 1934, gold wound up appreciating by an *identical* amount as the same basket of goods and services used in the CPI's calculation.

FIGURE 2.3 GOLD PRICE VS. THE PRICE LEVEL

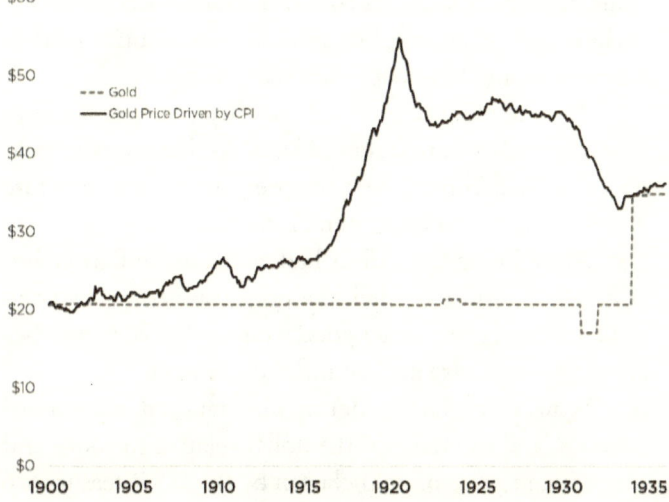

In the chart, the dotted line represents our theoretical price of gold. It's the price that gold would be at any moment if we simply let it appreciate every month in accordance with the CPI or a standard basket of goods and services. There's no black magic here.

We can also think of that dotted line as the rate of devaluation in the Dollar. Nearly every good got more expensive between 1900 and 1934, i.e. our paper dollars, even though they were backed by gold, became less valuable over that time. They bought fewer goods. For example, the price of a new home had nearly doubled between 1900 and the Great Depression. One needed nearly twice as many dollars to buy a house.

Under the gold standard, however, that price of one ounce of gold remained fixed at $20.67. For an entity like the U.S. government that held a large quantity of gold, its purchasing power slowly, steadily decreased. Until 1934, of course. Devaluing the Dollar by 40% and increasing the value of its gold holdings by a tremendous amount overnight sounds dramatic, but all it did was re-price gold to where it should have been that year to begin with.

After the Gold Reserve Act of 1934, the price of gold landed exactly where it should have. At that moment gold had increased in price over the previous 34 years at a rate almost identical to the general rate of inflation.

After being a terrible hedge against inflation between 1900 and *1933* when the price was artificially fixed at $20.67 and every other good went up in price, gold became a *perfect* hedge against inflation in 1934.

Now, to be fair, under a gold standard, the rate of inflation and the value of the dollar relative to goods and services and price of gold chosen by the US Treasury are all intimately linked. These variables are supposed to track over the long run.

In the case of the CPI and the value of the Dollar, it's true by definition. The CPI is how we quantify the change in the value of the Dollar. Love it or hate it, the CPI is designed to measure exactly how much less valuable our Dollars become relative to the goods and services they can purchase. In our study, all we're doing is using CPI data to model what it might look like if gold went up every year by the same amount that the Dollar went down.

Even though the CPI is one of the longest-running and most-reliable continuous data sets, it's worth point out a few important events in its history. For starters, the national CPI wasn't officially created until 1921. After that it was then backfilled with the same methodology to

1913 with official price data from various foods and consumer products. It was then estimated all the way back to 1800 by splicing in other historical price records.

It's an imperfect data set, so we must be mindful to expect some a certain degree of flexibility from these numbers. Gold appears to have magically landed exactly where it should have been priced in 1934. But if we used the same CPI methodology in those early years that we use today, it's possible that the intersection wouldn't be exact. It might only be close, instead.

But after the next few decades, we'll discover that none of that would even matter.

Chapter 6.

It's My Gold and I'll Value It How I Please

To a certain extent, gold was largely forgotten by the public in the years between Roosevelt and Nixon. We were still on a gold standard, of course. So it wasn't completely overlooked. It was still legal to own gold jewelry, as well, and for most citizens during this era, gold was simply materiel that was used for making shiny things to drape about our bodies. But owning gold in the form of bars or coins as an investment was illegal. And the relatively modern idea of thinking of gold as an investment would sound quite strange to a citizen from that era.

The U.S. Treasury defended that $35 peg for many years, buying from whomever and selling to approved central banks, intervening however and whenever to maintain the standard. The rest of us went about our lives.

But during the 1960's, this and other things in the country started to change. Everything else in the world had grown more expensive over the years. Wages. Cars. Orange juice. But again, not gold. Gold was still $35/oz. Gold had grown steadily more undervalued relative to assets with similar characteristics.

Things started changing culturally around gold, too. When we left the theater in 1964 after Ian Fleming's *Goldfinger*, we were hooked! Ft. Knox! We all wanted our own gold! It was coming back into the public eye. By the time inflation really started heating up in the late 1960's and 70's and the Dollar started receiving renewed criticism, the public started paying more attention to gold and where it's price *really* ought to be.

The mid 70's were an interesting time for a lot of reasons. But for gold, it was a truly revolutionary era. For the first time in everyone's lives the market had to figure out for itself at which price gold ought to settle. Gone were the days of the gold standard and an artificially fixed gold price.

This is when the second magical coincidence occurs.

FIGURE 2.4 GOLD PRICE VS. THE PRICE LEVEL

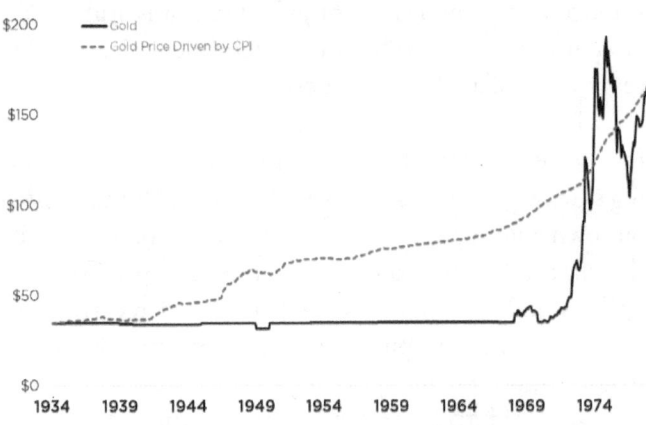

This chart is simply a continuation of the first. The solid line is the price of gold and the dotted line represents what the price of gold would be if it simply appreciated at the same rate of the CPI. In other words, it's what the price gold would be if it increased in value at the same rate that the Dollar decreased.

It's a remarkable occurrence. After decades of artificial suppression the price of gold was finally set free to float in the marketplace. Amazingly, the free market carried the price gold immediately to where it should have been priced all along. The free market got it exactly right.

It wasn't without volatility, of course. Volatility comes with the territory of every freely trading market, even the most liquid ones. Gold overshot, then undershot -- magically and coincidentally oscillating perfectly around this historical mean -- before hitting the price target on the nose again in 1977. Free markets may be messy, but historical evidence suggests that more often than not they work. They are efficient mechanisms for determining fair prices.

Our price chart looks simple, but there's a lot of back-story taking place behind those lines. After the post-War economic boom, the U.S. entered an era of turbulence in terms of global monetary policy. The only solution was to get off the gold standard. Eliminating the Dollar/gold peg didn't happen overnight, either. It was a process that unfolded over almost a full decade.

The first baby step happened in 1968 when the Sterling price was abandoned in London. That left the Dollar as the final and formal basis for the gold price. At the same time, gold was allowed to float freely in special private markets, while only central banks could trade with the U.S. at the $35 peg.

The next step was the biggest. In 1971, President Nixon officially ended the international convertibility of the Dollar to gold. The post-WWII Bretton Woods system, which pegged the world's major currencies to the U.S. Dollar, and by extension, gold, came to an end. Dollars no longer had value because they were backed by a specified amount of gold. Dollars now had value "by fiat." They had value because the government said they did. Perhaps more importantly, Dollars had value because they could always be used to settle one's tax debts with the government.

After 1971, the price of gold was allowed to float freely in nearly every market around the world.

The last key step toward getting off the gold standard didn't occur until 1975. It wasn't until then that U.S. citizens were finally free to own gold in any form without any restrictions. The idea of gold as an investment and independent asset class was born.

As we return to our basic price model that uses the rate of inflation to predict the price of gold, we see some convincing evidence linking the two. The price of gold closed that year at $140.75 per ounce. If, for the previous 75 years, the price of gold was instead determined by the rate of inflation, it would have closed that year at $145.34 per ounce.

After seven decades of a gold standard, artificial price suppression at two different pegs, and five full years of freely floating prices, gold closed right where one would have expected. The free market had gotten it almost exactly right. Our framework appears correct. Increases in the price of gold should be equivalent to decreases in the value of the paper currency in which gold is denominated.

This is where our story starts to get interesting. By the end of the decade, Gold prices would get out of control, culminating in a massive bubble. Bubbles are another unfortunate side effect of freely trading markets. Like any bubble in history, the stratospheric gold price seemed sensible at the time, especially against the backdrop of U.S. hyper-inflation. It didn't matter that the price of gold went up much more than the Dollar went down. The price of gold was now being pushed around by speculators. Gone was the sexiness & glamor of *Goldfinger*, replaced instead by the fear & desperation chronicled by Paddy Chayefsky's *Network*. Our hunger for gold was now motivated by a far more powerful driver.

To an observer at the time, it seemed as though gold and inflation were going to decouple for good. The one seemed to have nothing to do with the other. Inflation may have been running hot in the 70's and early 80's, but gold prices were incendiary. They seemed to have no upper bounds. Investors could only speculate how much worse the inflation was going to get.

The power and history embedded in this gold-inflation model were too great, however.

This wouldn't be the last time that gold and inflation would intersect.

Chapter 7.

PUTTING THE FREE MARKET TO THE TEST

When we think of gold, we think of a rich, thousand-year history. We think of it as being inseparable from our classic concepts of currency. But what we forget is that much of this is strictly a modern convention and a retroactive re-writing of the way that things actually were. For a large chunk of the U.S. history, gold existed outside the public eye. Nobody cared except the wonks and the central banks. We had a gold standard, but the way most of us think about gold today – as a currency, investment, or asset class – would have seemed completely foreign to someone 50-75 years ago.

History isn't just about fact, it's about perception. It's about what happens, but also how we interpret its meaning. The way that perception and cultural narratives quietly shift over time is an occasionally-insidious factor that is perpetually under-appreciated in the present. It's why history and our understanding of it seems to change as time moves on.

Since gold started trading freely on the open market – and especially when it became possible to trade gold in the equity market through ETFs – both our perception of it and its price behavior have changed dramatically. The long term trend is still the same. Gold still rise over the long run at the rate of inflation. Over the short run, however, we see more of that inevitable side effect of free markets: volatility.

Here's what our model looks like when we reset our inflation clock to 1973 and run it through the end of 2005.

FIGURE 2.5 GOLD PRICE VS. THE PRICE LEVEL

Again, there's no black magic here. This is simply the market price of gold and what the theoretical price of gold should be if we let it rise in accordance with inflation rate. It's what the price of gold should be if it appreciated at the same rate the Dollar depreciated.

During the bubble of 1981, gold seemed to have completely decoupled. But this is what happens during bubbles. They are momentary periods of speculative excess. They're driven by behavior and psychology, not fundamentals.

Like every other bubble in history, it didn't last. The price of gold crashed. Eventually fundamentals – the rate of inflation – started mattering again. Gold prices went up and down and ultimately nowhere between the early 1980's and the mid 1990's. Meanwhile, inflation chugged on and the value of the Dollar steadily declined. Eventually, these trends and prices all met again, just as they had so many times in the century before. The lives of gold and the Dollar were technically independent, but intimately linked, evidenced by an ongoing series of moonlight rendezvous, magically overlapping for a moment or two before heading off in their separate directions.

During the mid 90's, it appeared as though gold and the Dollar would settled down for good. At last, it seemed as though the two might move together in lockstep. Gold and inflation each appreciated by an almost identical amount for most of the decade. But the marriage would be brief, and in 1996 gold and the Dollar would break up yet again.

During the late 90's, nearly everyone would fall out of love with gold. It was the era of the technology boom, online brokers, and democratized investing. Other assets boomed as well. Seemingly every asset. Bonds, real estate, foreign stocks, currencies. Gold was left for dead, and for the first time since its price was artificially suppressed under the gold standard, gold traded far below the price suggested by our inflation-based model. In August of 1999 the price of gold closed at $254, nearly *half* of what the price of gold should have been. In a lot of ways, gold was in a "negative bubble" during this period. It traded at an irrational low relative to its trend while every other asset class in the world soared to remarkable, all-time highs.

That wouldn't last either, of course. As prices tend to do, gold would eventually revert to its historical mean. By 2005, the price of the gold and the value of the Dollar would meet again for one last fling.

Keep in mind this trendline is still the exact same one that we started way back in 1900.

After 105 years, the price of gold had risen by the exact amount that the Dollar had fallen.

After 105 years, gold wasn't just a good hedge against inflation, it was a *perfect* hedge against inflation.

It's worth pointing out that 2005 was an interesting year as well. If I came to you with this study back then, you would have said that this all makes pretty good sense. You'd think that using the inflation rate as a basic long-term proxy about which the gold price ought to oscillate would be really clever. That's assuming I could have distracted you long enough from your condo flipping to listen for a minute or two. You also would have conceded that gold was way too cheap in 2001 and way too expensive in the early 80's. You would have said that today, in the year 2005, gold was probably fairly valued. Our trend-based approach seems reasonable.

It's not perfect, though. There are obviously a lot problems with this inflation-based framework in that gold can overshoot its trend line dramatically. Under this study, gold should have been worth a little more than $200 in 1980, but we all know what happened in the midst of that bubble. At the peak, it had overshot its historical trend by a factor of *four*. While the gold bubble of

1980 is one of the dominant events in its history, what we've largely forgotten is how quickly it fell back to "fair value." By 1985 it was more or less there. Mean reversion is a powerful thing.

Gold isn't the only asset that overshoots and undershoots. Stocks do it too. Equity prices have reached some equally crazy extremes in their history. Think about how rich valuations were in 1929 or 2000. Or how irrationally cheap stocks were in the early 80's. These valuations can persist for a little while, but they too revert to mean. Even real estate, as slow-moving an asset class as there is, reached an unbelievable peak, then fell far below its historical trend before rising back up to fair value.

Asset prices can move all over the place. But as long as we know what the underlying trend is, and which key factors drive the price of an asset, we can understand where current prices are in relation to it. We can know whether current prices are too expensive or too cheap, or if the asset is fairly valued.

This simple trend-based model may seem to work really well over long windows of time, but never forget that all sorts of wild things can happen in the markets. It can get even worse with gold, too, a market that's tiny compared to the size of the equity, bond, and real estate markets.

Despite all that noise, one way or another, prices inevitably fall (or rise) back to what the historical trend suggests.

Chapter 8.

A Re-Writing of Gold's History

One more thing we've forgotten to appreciate is how remarkably the gold narrative changed after the financial crisis in 2008. That's when a number of factors had finally come together for gold:

Good momentum. Between 2001 and 2007 gold increased at an astonish rate of over 17% per year. By early 2008, it had attracted the attention of investors large and small, finally held in favor after nearly 3 decades in the dog house. As we learned from our earlier study, a large portion of the move from the mid $200s to almost $1,000/oz was simple mean reversion. But trends never stop at fair value. They are invariably carried above and beyond to a new local extreme.

Easier access. Perhaps the most important innovation in the modern history of the gold market was the exchange traded fund. In November of 2004, State Street Global Advisors launched the GLD fund. It traded on the New York Stock Exchange. Now investors could get access to the gold bullion market via the *stock* market. Gone was the hassle of storing the physical commodity and the logistical and administrative complexities of trading in the futures markets. It opened the doors for millions of retail investors to participate in a market that most had never participated in. In the years that followed, several other exchange traded gold products would launch, giving investors many different ways to invest in gold. After a few years of strong performance and no more barriers to entry, investors happily jumped on board, fueling the ongoing ascent of gold prices.

A need for a new asset class. During the financial crisis of 2008, multiple asset classes collapsed together. Real estate, stocks, international stocks, junk bonds, even certain good quality bonds all suffered extreme losses. Terrified, investors had no place to go aside from cash. After watching all these assets fail simultaneously, investors began demanding a new asset class, one whose returns weren't linked to the economic performance that underpinned other risk assets. Many of these investors found comfort in gold.

The inflation meme. After the high-profile corporate bailouts, sharp increase in government borrowing, and quantitative easing programs from the Federal Reserve, investors began fretting about potential future inflation. The last time the public had been infatuated with gold was during the hyper-inflationary 1970's. Investors who were convinced that the U.S. Dollar would lose much of its purchasing power in the years ahead fled to the gold market.

Distrust in central banks and government institutions. Tangential to worries about the potential failure of the Dollar was a new round of distrust in governments and global monetary authorities. Inspired by the potential protection that gold offered from these "untrustworthy" and "profligate" entities, investors who had historically ignored gold began incorporating it into their investment portfolios. A certain pocket of public, led by figures such as Ron Paul, even expressed desire to return to the gold standard.

Cultural changes. Doomsday prepping and worries (or dark fantasies) about apocalyptic scenarios, financial and otherwise. The more investors that bought for cultural reasons, the higher the price went.

During the early post-crisis years, gold was no longer just a thing. It had become woven into the fabric of who many of us were as individuals. It symbolized our beliefs and fiscal values. Sentiment about gold was almost the polar opposite from the early 2000s.

✠

None of these factors had existed in the decades prior. A decade prior, there was no bullish trend in gold, nor was there an easy way for investors to access it, nor was there a need for a new and uncorrelated asset class that could theoretically offer protection against a collapse in the U.S. Dollar in a way that other asset classes couldn't. A decade prior, investors were happy with the economy and the way it was being managed. They were happy with the Dollars in which everything was denominated.

As these factors all came together in unison, they stoked investor demand for gold higher and higher. Between November of 2008 and August of 2011, gold would appreciate at an eye-popping rate of 37.8% per year. It was a phenomenon that transcended traditional financial boundaries and ran rampant through popular culture. Everyone from investment pundits to taxi drivers was talking about gold.

What's more is that these psychological changes and the resurgence in gold's price helped re-write the way we thought about gold. The historical narrative was retroactively re-written.

People who had never paid attention before started to.

So where does that put us today?

FIGURE 2.6 GOLD PRICE VS. THE PRICE LEVEL

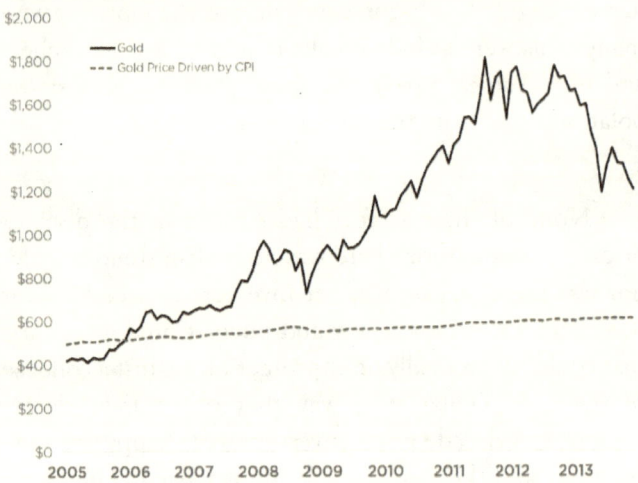

Under our basic inflation/Dollar model, the "fair price" of gold is quite a ways lower still.

The idea of setting gold to appreciate in accordance with the inflation rate – or *inversely* to the Dollars in which it is denominated – may have sounded absurd at first. If I'd come to you with this story in 2011 when gold was approaching $2,000/oz, even the gold skeptics would have dismissed me outright.

Even today, there's a good chance that many would still dismiss this notion of using the inflation rate as a long-term trend line about which the price of gold out to fluctuate. There's no small amount of irony here, too, as those most willing to dismiss this notion today are also the ones who adamantly believe that gold prices are going much, much higher because of future hyper-inflation. After reflecting on some historical data, it's clear that inflation has quite a ways to still catch up.

You can see, though, that if I'd told you right off the bat that an ounce of gold today should be worth $600-$800/oz, even the most bearish investors would have laughed me out of the room. Nobody would have heard me out.

Now that we've calmly walked through the last century, the idea of using an inflation-based trend line for gold's price doesn't sound so crazy, does it? After all, our original premise was that gold, an asset that doesn't generate earnings or pay a dividend, should by definition increase in price at a rate equal to the rate at which the paper currencies in which gold is denominated *decrease* in price. In other words: gold should over the long run appreciate at the rate of inflation. Even if it sounds like a sensible framework in an academic sense, the conclusions of this framework are still uncomfortable to many.

If the last 5 years had never happened would we be so quick to reject such a thesis? I doubt it.

We can twist this perspective a bit to state it a different way. Gold has appreciated at an astonishing rate in the post-crisis years. By simply looking at the last decade, the idea of using the inflation rate as a long-term trend would seem absurd. But by looking at the last century's worth of history and data, the idea of using the inflation rate as a long-term trend seems like the only sensible thing.

Rejecting this notion, and by extension, the conclusion that the gold price is well above what it ought to be, is contingent on a specific set events happening in the future. To justify today's gold prices, the Dollar must fall in value – substantially – in the years to come. There needs to be hyperinflation in the *future*. There needs to be a *future* monetary collapse. That's the only thing that could reconcile today's gold prices with their historical trend. Aside from a plunge in the *gold* price, of course.

In a way, this is somewhat revealing about our deeper psychology. It's as though we are subconsciously conceding the point that current prices have disconnected themselves from history and require specific *future* outcomes to justify themselves.

But if there's no hyperinflation or global monetary collapse, then what?

Unfortunately, we don't get to pick and choose which characteristics of gold are ancient. If we're willing to tell stories about that are thousands of years old about gold, we can't be so quick to ignore crucial aspects of its history that occurred within just the last century.

FIGURE 2.7 GOLD PRICE VS. THE PRICE LEVEL

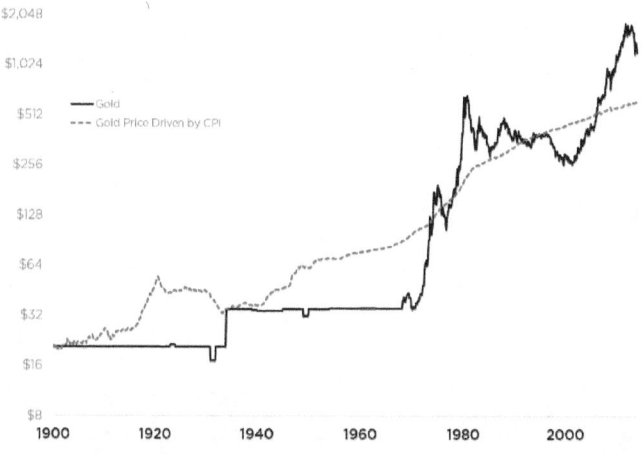

There are investors out there who believe the price of gold is going to $5,000/oz and beyond. For the most part, these opinions aren't given much credence by the broader marketplace. You can see why. That kind of outcome requires one of two outcomes: a massive and unprecedented collapse in the Dollar or accepting that notion that gold prices have nothing to do with inflation.

In general, gold bulls tend to believe rather passionately that gold and inflation are intimately linked. And, in fact, the data suggest that over the long run they are. Therefore, a future collapse in the world's paper currencies is the only way in which today's above-trend prices can be justified.

And what if that never happens?

Chapter 9.

CAVEATS APLENTY

Obviously, there are all sorts of problems with this type of framework. It isn't just the rate of inflation that moves the price of gold around.

To start, this study does nothing to account for supply and demand the gold market. These are the forces that move the price of every asset up and down. These forces can impact prices over the short-term in the form of supply shocks and demand spikes. Short-term distortions always revert to trend over time, however. It is the long-term supply and demand for gold that govern price.

On the **demand** side of the curve, I'm not sure there's anyone on the planet that understands the true demand for gold and the way it intersects with supply. What is the aggregate demand for gold? We know how much gold central banks around the world buy. We can see the flows going into and out of institutional entities such as the exchange traded gold funds or mutual funds. But what governs this? What makes a government or the public want to buy or sell gold? It's a massively complex array of factors.

One of those factors – perhaps the most important – is gold's price. In a sense, when we feel that the price of gold is too expensive, we stay away. Demand cools; prices flatten or fall. When gold gets sufficiently cheap, demand stirs. Fresh demand pushes prices up.

With an asset like gold that literally doesn't do anything except sit there, price influences demand as much or more than demand influences price. This isn't like the latest iPhone or a stick of deodorant where we can get a fairly accurate read on a level of demand that's largely independent of price. Whether or not we choose to buy or sell gold has as much to do with plain old price as anything.

Between those poles of "too expensive" and "too cheap" are two other factors: momentum and the inflation rate. One sets the basic long-term trajectory while the other drives the oscillation about it. Demand, meanwhile, is what determines how far in one direction we're willing to allow those prices to oscillate.

On the **supply** side, gold is also interesting and unique. We produce six times as much gold per year today than we did in the year 1900 (with five times the global population). The amount of gold produced has also fluctuated over time and this too is influenced by the price. When gold prices are high, it makes sense to mine gold from expensive locations. This increases future supply which has a naturally depressing effect on price. When prices are low, it doesn't make sense for gold producers to spend more to mine an ounce of gold than they can sell it for. Supply slows. And as supply slows relative to demand, prices naturally rise. The way that price governs supply is another reason why gold tends to move in long, strange cycles.

Another unique quality of the gold supply is that its global stock is never really used up. It simply changes hands and form. Gold isn't consumed the way that commodities like corn, crude oil, or even copper are. We don't dig it up and make it disappear through our use. Gold also can't go out of business and disappear the way a corporation can. It can't default. Every year the total supply increases.

With an asset like crude oil, it makes sense to assume quantum leaps in its "fair value". The average cost to produce a barrel of crude oil is significantly more expensive than it was 20 years ago, much more than the corresponding increase in the inflation rate over that time. And it's with good reason, too. Like untapped gold reserves, today's crude oil supplies are in difficult, expensive places to reach. Crude can't trade at $25 for very long before the supply dries up and prices leap higher.

The oil we pumped in 1994 is long gone; we've gotta go back to the ground to get more. But all the gold that man has ever mined is, more or less, still with us. It's yet one more way why gold doesn't work the way other commodities do and it's why the fundamentals behind supply and demand matter less.

If every gold company in the world shut off their mines, there's no reason price should spike the way it would with consumable commodities. Obviously, that kind of event would spike for short-term psychological reasons. But would it be justified and sustainable over a longer window of time? I've got some gold. I'll happily trade it to you for Dollars at a price somewhere sufficiently higher than here. And I'm sure you'd trade it to someone else for a price sufficiently higher than that. And that gold won't ever go anywhere. We'll just swap it back and forth. Nothing on the supply side will ever prevent us from trading gold for Dollars and Dollars for gold. We can do this indefinitely.

The supply doesn't have to be switched off to reach a point where the current stock starts changing hands. Price will do it on its own. At the peak of gold's ascent in 2011, a new cottage industry developed. It was devoted to buying gold jewelry and dental fillings from the public. Individuals from all walks of life – not just those investing in the capital markets – were in effect expressing their own views about the current gold price. They believed that at over $1,500/oz, they would rather have cash than gold. By extension, they did not believe that gold was likely to continue appreciating, else, being rational individuals, they would have held onto the gold and let it appreciate. They did this even if they weren't explicitly aware of doing so.

If you think about it, the moment those "we buy gold" signs became ubiquitous was it. That marked an important peak – a cyclical peak if not a generational one. Almost by definition, that was the turning point. That was when supply from a previously fixed location began flooding back into the market. That was the moment when the feedback loop started bending back the other way.

There's another major caveat in this study. We've used the rate of inflation in the United States and the value of the U.S. Dollar as the basis of our study. But gold is a *global* asset. For the 70 years under the gold standard, that obviously didn't matter. The gold and the Dollar were explicitly linked. Nor did it matter much in the decade or two shortly thereafter, while the U.S. dominated the gold market.

Today and over the last few decades, what happens in the gold market is a function of global variables. It is global demand and sentiment that determines momentum, and it is the value of the global currencies in which gold is denominated that govern the long-term trend in price.

Fortunately, we have some great data on this. The Organization for Economic Co-operation and Development (OECD) publishes inflation data for the G20 nations all the way back to 1996. The world's 20 largest economies don't encompass everything, but these countries represent a big enough portion of the $45 trillion global economy that it's a good enough place to start. What happens in those countries' economies and with their currencies is largely reflective of the planet as a whole.

As it happens, the rate of inflation at the global level over the last two decades has been a little higher than in the United States. The global average annual rate of inflation between 1996 and 2013 was 3.9% versus the 2.4% in the U.S. As countries like China and India have begun demanding more gold for their own unique reasons, we should incorporate the effect of that as we establish a revised basis for the long-term price trend. We can take this global inflation data and update our original model.

We redraw our graph as follows:

FIGURE 2.8 GOLD PRICE VS. THE GLOBAL PRICE LEVEL

Using the U.S. Consumer Price Index from 1900 to 1996 and the OECD's aggregate G20 inflation rate from 1996 to the end of 2013, we can calculate a "fair value" for gold of $812.

$812 per ounce.

If we assume, sensibly, that gold should appreciate in price at the rate by which the global currencies in which it is denominated decrease in value, that's what gold ought to be worth. Every year as the world's currencies get less valuable gold should become slightly more valuable. This is the long-term trend, and as we've seen, over long windows of time, it's a very sensible trend-driver. It works for legitimate fundamental reasons, even if the noise in the gold market on a year-to-year basis is as cacophonous as it gets.

It's possible that $812/oz at the end of 2013 is still a bit generous. Low inflation countries like the U.S. and Germany own an overwhelming portion of the world's gold supply and the world's #3 and #4 buyers respectively. But higher inflation countries like India and China are the world's #1 and #2 buyers, so it's clear that a strictly U.S CPI-based model is inappropriate.

Ultimately, the details don't matter as much as the big picture. It's impossible to determine the fair price of gold with precision, and even if we could, it's unlikely that the market price for gold would stay there for very long. Gold is constantly moving in one direction and its rate of movement is over the short-run is almost always faster than inflation. Investors are a short-sighted lot.

No matter what the environment – artificial price suppression under a gold standard, a volatile free market, or psychological bubbles – gold has simply been unable to deviate too far from this basic driver. Inflation may be the chain to gold's shiny ball, but the two have only intersected around a dozen times in the last 114 years.

Even though a basic framework like this lacks detail and precision. It is extremely helpful for determining if gold prices are too high or too low in general. This type of model has a lengthy and impressive track record of success for doing so.

In order to say that this model doesn't work and that it fails to identify the moments at which gold is too expensive or too cheap – including today – one has to say that something else drives the long-term gold price or that gold *does* something else. Which it doesn't, of course. Only 10% of all the gold mined gets used for industrial purposes. The rest goes to jewelry, coins, and bars. Gold doesn't generate earnings and it doesn't even really deplete; it simply stores value as the currencies in which it is denominated decrease in value.

The Religion of Gold

I think this is why so many smart people on both sides of the discussion think of gold as a "neutral currency."

Caveats Aplenty

PART 3

A BASIC PROJECTION MODEL

Chapter 10.

Estimating Future Returns

Now that we've established a framework for understanding what drives the price of gold – randomness over the short run and inflation over the long run – we can start feeding some of this basic data into a basic model.

This isn't as complicated as it sounds. Estimating future prices is actually quite simple. On a day-to-day or even a year-to-year basis it's impossible to do with accuracy, of course. During any given day or year, markets are driven by noise and chaos and fickle factors like sentiment and momentum. Those near-term forces are incredibly difficult to model or even understand. But over very long windows of time, it's not just possible, but rather quite simple to project how much an asset will increase or decrease in value. Building a model that does this is almost trivial.

Investors have been using these types of models to project future prices for a long time. Legendary, highly-respected investors like Jeremy Grantham and John

Hussman have written about these extensively[17]. Every investment bank around the world has their own set of internal models that use similar inputs and attempt to project future long-term returns.

Most price projection models like this are based on the same basic idea: assets rise and fall because of fundamental reasons and psychological reasons. The fundamental reasons are what determine an assets value over longer windows of time. They establish the basic secular trend. The psychological reasons are what move prices around over shorter windows of time. Psychology is what pushes solid investments to distressed valuations. It's what drives risky investments to bubble levels.

On the fundamental side, the market valuation for any company is ultimately based on the level of profits that company generates, a theoretically endless stream of future cash flows. By discounting all those future cash flows to today we can get a sense of how much it ought to be worth. As those cash flows change relative to our expectations and profitability grows or shrink, the company's value changes. This is an example of a fundamental value driver.

Over the long run, the entire U.S. stock market tends to appreciate at a rate that can be decomposed into the following formula:

```
GDP + Dividends + Inflation
```

Those are the primary fundamental components of the market's return. Investors receive economic growth

---

[17] "Estimating the Long-Term Return on Stocks." *Hussman Econometrics*. Web. June 1998.

in the form of growing corporate earnings, direct dividend payouts, and a higher price level by way of inflation.

During certain environments, investor psychology will influence how much more (or less) the market should be worth relative to its historical norms. During hopeful and bullish cultural and macro-economic environments, investors are willing to take more risk and pay a higher price per unit of expected profit. In more anxious economic climates, investors become risk averse and will not pay high prices for a dollar of future earnings. This psychology is what causes markets to get expensive or cheap relative to their historical norms.

The same valuation concept applies to gold.

With gold, as we established in Part 2, the trend driver is simply the rate of inflation. Or rather, the *inverse* value of all the paper currencies in which gold is denominated. As paper currencies go down in value, gold goes up in value. By definition, those two factors are identical; inflation is precisely how we measure the decrease in value of a currency relative to a fixed basket of goods.

The amount of this devaluation is equal to the long-term average rate of appreciation in gold. The inflation rate is the trend. How far gold gets above or below that trend due to psychological factors impacts the degree of returns that investors will actually experience. When gold is overvalued relative to trend, future returns will be lower as prices revert back towards their mean. When gold is undervalued relative to trend, future returns will be higher as prices revert back towards their mean.

Let's now recall our chart from the previous section, the one that relates the current price of gold to its long-term trend.

FIGURE 3.1 GOLD PRICE VS. THE GLOBAL PRICE

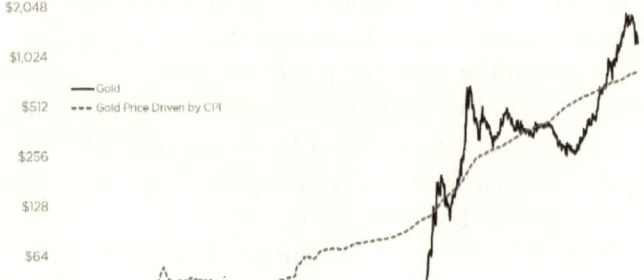

As of the end of 2013, our inflation-based model was suggesting a "fair value" for gold of $812 per ounce.

What gold will do this year or next is anybody's guess. But we have a much better idea where gold prices will go over the next *decade*. That's a long enough window such that the short-term noise will even out. It's also long enough to observe how the basic trend moves and how the gold price oscillates in huge cycles around it. Given what we know about the fundamental characteristics of gold, the probability that this pattern continues in the future is a virtual guarantee. Prices can only go so far above or below trend. It would be highly unlikely, for example, to see gold prices rose to $5,000/oz over the next decade, at least as long as the current inflation-based trend stays in place.

Since the U.S. was on a gold standard or gold exchange standard for 70 years, it doesn't make much sense to use a price projection model like this before 1974. The price was artificially suppressed at a fixed level and a model to project future prices was ineffective and unecessary. In addition, the public couldn't even own gold as an investment until January 1975 anyway. So that's where we'll start our model. Since this will be a 10-year forward model, we'll incorporate the prior decade's worth of data as an input.

The way this model works is simple. It uses our historical data about gold prices and the inflation rate to estimate how much gold will go up or down over the coming decade. In Figure 3.2, this is the dotted line. It's the *projected* rate of return for gold over the next ten years. Our model makes this estimate once per month and then simply logs these projections in the form of a line.

During the early- and mid-1970's, our model was projecting very high future performance for gold. By 1980, our model was suggesting that future returns would be very poor. Our model was suggesting that investors who bought during the gold bubble would not be rewarded over the coming decade.

You can see, of course, that they weren't.

Estimating Future Returns

FIGURE 3.3 PREDICTING FUTURE RETURNS IN GOLD

In Figure 3.4, the solid line is equal to the actual rate of returns that investors earned over the coming decade. The dotted line is what our model predicted.

As an example, at the end of 1980, shortly after the bubble in gold had burst, our model suggested that investors would earn an average rate of return of -4.8% per year over the coming decade. They actually wound up earning -4.2%.

For the most part, this model does a good job. The correlation between these two lines is 93%. It doesn't always forecast returns with precision, but if you're searching for precision with a decade-long model like this, the only thing you'll find is disappointment. Instead we have to settle for "close enough," which is quite acceptable as far as long-term investors are concerned. It suggested that buying gold during the wild gold enthusiasm of the early 1980's would be a terrible idea, and indeed it was. It suggested that buying in the late 80's or mid 90's would generate lackluster future returns, and that's what wound up happening.

Our model is also eerily effective at pointing out the moments of extremity. By 2001, gold was among the most hated asset classes in the world. Quite possibly *the* most hated. This model was suggesting, however, that one should be buying gold hand over fist. It was a moment of extremity, the exact psychological opposite of the bubble mindset of the early 80's. And as it happened, that was an excellent moment in history to buy gold. Quite possibly the *best* moment. Investors enjoyed substantial profits over the coming decade, returns that were well above the historical average for gold.

Perhaps more relevant for today's investors, the model was suggesting that early 2011 was among the *worst* moments in history in which to buy gold. Prices in 2011 almost touched $2,000/oz. The only time gold had ever been more overvalued relative to its 100+ year trend was in 1980, a moment at which the entire world now accepts as the peak of an irrational bubble. Like 1980, the year 2011 also represented a moment at which investor enthusiasm about gold was at highs not seen in ages. We've only got a few years of actual data so far, but with gold down roughly 40% from those highs, investors who listened to the warning sounded by this model and avoided or sold gold in 2011 are probably glad that they did. Sentiment seems mixed, however. For the most part, the idea that 2011 represented a bubble in gold isn't widely accepted. Old ghosts are always given up slowly.

With a price of $1,200/oz at the end of 2013 relative to a target "fair value" of $812/oz, our model is suggesting disappointing future returns for gold. It's projecting an average annual rate of return of -1.8%. We obviously can't say for sure what will happen. But we'll check back in the year 2023 and see where the market is. Based on the way this model has performed in the past, it's almost certain that returns will be somewhere in the range of -4% to +2% per year.

I should note that this model carries a large and important caveat. It's dependent on our knowledge of the future. The "projected returns" here all assume that you know what the inflation rate over the subsequent decade is going to look like.

This is where it gets interesting. Thirty or forty years ago, the future rate of inflation was anyone's guess. In fact, in the 70's and 80's, you can see how important it was, as a gold investor, to be able to predict what the future inflation rate was going to be. If you knew what forward rate of inflation was going to be, you knew almost exactly how much money you were going to make in gold. It's remarkable how closely those two variables tracked.

Inflation was tough to predict back then, however. Who would have guessed in 1973 that inflation was going to average nearly 9% over the coming decade? And who expected in 1982 that inflation actually would get back under control? Investors who accurately predicted that and used that knowledge in the gold market had great success.

In the chart, it stands out that this model starts breaking down and becoming substantially less precise around 1987. Coincidentally, that was the year that Alan Greenspan assumed chairmanship of the Federal Reserve. The Greenspan Fed will be remembered for a lot of reasons, but one in particular is that while Greenspan and his modern successors have been at the helm, inflation has become incredibly easy to forecast. And it's become remarkably stable as well. This is probably because one of the Federal Reserve's explicit mandates is price stability. The Fed wants inflation to run at a certain stable rate every year, never falling too low or rising too high. They're very clear about this in every speech and every testimony. For the most part, with the tools available to them in their policy chest, they're able to accomplish this. Since 1987, their track record at keeping inflation constrained in a relatively tight window is exceptional. Only briefly has the rate of inflation since then fallen below 0% or risen above 5%. They are very communicative about this policy and their current targets. Greater transparency is another hallmark of the modern Fed.

Additionally, there are mechanisms today that allow us to use the markets to get a read on what long-term inflation will look like. Treasury Inflation Protected Securities (TIPS) are relatively new invention. TIPS are government bonds that adjust how much interest they pay based on the inflation rate. They change their value every year in accordance with the Consumer Price Index. As inflation rises, the interest payments grow. As inflation contracts, the payments shrink.

If you want to get a sense of what the market thinks the rate of inflation is going to be over the coming decade, all one has to do is relate TIPS to regular Treasury bonds. Simply compare the current yield on 10yr TIPS with the current yield on straight Treasuries. The difference is what the market, in aggregate, thinks inflation is going to look like over the coming decade.

At the end of 2013, this projected rate of inflation was around 2% per year. This also happens to be squarely inside the Federal Reserve's range for the targeted rate of inflation.

Our model is using *global* inflation, so the projected rate of inflation should be a little higher, of course, somewhere in the neighborhood of 3%. This becomes the starting point for what will drive the price of gold over the next decade. This is the baseline for the trend in the gold price.

If global inflation does wind up averaging 3% over the next decade, the odds that our projected performance for gold matches the actual performance improve significantly. If inflation winds up averaging 10% over the next decade (or 0%), our model and its assumption of 3% global inflation will likely miss its targets for how much gold will return.

If anything, these kinds of studies are a refreshing reminder of how little we know about the future and how little precision we have when trying to forecast it. A model like this is about as good as we can do, and as you can see, there's an honest argument to be made that it's not even good enough to be useful for real investors making real investment decisions.

Imperfections aside, there is some value in the sense that this kind of model, like its brethren in the equity space, does a great job helping you spot the moments at which future returns are going to be generally good and the moments at which future returns will be generally terrible. If gold ever gets too far above or below its historical trend, this model will sound the alarm just as it has for the last 114 years.

PART 4

THE SEVEN THINGS EVERY INVESTOR NEEDS TO KNOW ABOUT GOLD

The Religion of Gold

Because of all the dogma and oft-recited talking points associated with gold, there are more than a few misconceptions about it. The first step toward investment success is being able to see the playing field with clear eyes.

Understanding why gold behaves the way that it does is difficult. Some say it's impossible. Gold is its own animal and it does things its own way. We know that over the long run, it tends to be intimately linked to the rate of inflation and the purchasing power of the global currencies in which it is denominated. Over shorter windows of time – and windows of a decade or less fall within this category – anything can happen. Literally any outcome is in play.

The following points won't unlock the secret mysteries of gold. Man has been trying and failing to understand those mysteries for millennia. The Religion of Gold arguably contains as much "magic" as any other dimension of our culture.

These evidence-based and data-supported concepts will, however, help you establish a better framework for trying to make sense of all the noise in the marketplace. They are all incontrovertibly true, even though many forget or neglect these truths from time to time.

Understanding these ideas in full will help you make better decisions and develop better expectations about what happens between today, tomorrow, and a foggy, undefined future.

Chapter 11.

GOLD DOESN'T DO ANYTHING

Today the world's gold stock is about 170,000 metric tons. If all of this gold were melded together, it would form a cube of about 68 feet per side. (Picture it fitting comfortably within a baseball infield.) At $1,750 per ounce -- gold's price as I write this -- its value would be $9.6 trillion. Call this cube pile A.

Let's now create a pile B costing an equal amount. For that, we could buy all U.S. cropland (400 million acres with output of about $200 billion annually), plus 16 Exxon Mobils (the world's most profitable company, one earning more than $40 billion annually). After these purchases, we would have about $1 trillion left over for walking-around money (no sense feeling strapped after this buying binge). Can you imagine an investor with $9.6 trillion selecting pile A over pile B?

A century from now the 400 million acres of farmland will have produced staggering amounts of corn, wheat, cotton, and other crops -- and will continue to produce that valuable bounty, whatever the currency may be. Exxon Mobil will probably have delivered trillions of dollars in dividends to its owners and will also hold assets worth many more trillions (and, remember, you get 16 Exxons). The 170,000 tons of gold will be unchanged in size and still incapable of producing anything.

The Religion of Gold

You can fondle the cube, but it will not respond.

- Warren Buffet, excerpted from his 2011 shareholder letter.

This is perhaps the most important point to consider of all. It's the concept that frames everything else we know about gold.
Gold doesn't do anything.
It doesn't generate earnings.
It doesn't grow.
It doesn't pay you a dividend.
It gets dug up out of a hole in the ground in Africa or in my home state of Nevada. We melt it down, refine it, and change its form into something more portable and attractive. Various parties buy it for various reasons. More often than not, it winds up back in a hole of sorts where someone is paid to stand around and guard it. And there it will sit, in its safe deposit box, vault, or underground shelter, doing nothing.

The reason why this point is worth understanding is because *compounding* – growth upon growth – is one of the critical components of long-term investment returns.

Companies pay shareholders dividends which can be reinvested into the company to earn more dividends in the future. Cash flow generated by real estate can be redeployed into the purchase of additional real estate, which generates more cash flow which lets you buy even more real estate. Even cash compounds, or, rather, before the Fed's "zero interest rate policy" in the post-2008 years, cash used to compound. The marginal interest one earns in one year is subject to additional gains in the future years. Compounding is a massively powerful force.

Gold enjoys none of those benefits. There is no compounding with gold.

Beyond tangible cash flow, most investments do something or grant specific privileges. A share of stock entitles an investor to a portion of the stream of earnings that a company generates. A house, apartment complex, or office park can be lived in or rented out. Having a roof over one's head or the option to establish an additional stream of cash flow are benefits whose value hold up over time and can even appreciate.

Even if we expand our definition of "investment" to include something slightly more abstract like a college degree, it's a designation that confers concrete benefits in the marketplace and enables one to secure a higher salary than one might otherwise be able to earn.

Gold does none of these things either.

By extension, thinking of gold as an investment can be a dangerous proposition. It fails many of the tests that define something as an investment.

In fact, thinking of gold as a "negative investment" is an interesting perspective to consider. Historically, some of gold's best performance came during environments when relatively few other investments in the world were going up. The U.S. stock market lost over 50% between October 2007 and February 2009. International stock markets experience similar fates. U.S. Treasury bonds performed well as investors sought a safe haven, but bonds of lesser quality struggled and in the case of junk bonds, experienced massive losses[18]. Real estate continued its post-bubble slide during those years, with the

---

[18] A popular junk bond fund, the SPDR Barclays High Yield Bond Fund (ticker: JNK), lost 33% between December 2007 and February 2009.

S&P/Case-Shiller Home Price Index falling 24%. As all these other investments around the world were dropping, gold gained over 20% during that window.

The 1970's were another time when traditional investments floundered while gold performed quite well. By the early 1980's, global stock, bond, and real estate markets were all about to begin a massive 20 year bull market. Gold, of course, fell in value during that window.

There's not enough data to support the idea that gold should always be relied upon to perform well when traditional asset classes aren't. Gold's long-term monthly correlation with the stock market is 0.009. Its correlation with real estate is -0.09. Statistically, this means that what happens to gold in any given month has nothing to do with what happens in any other asset class.

Gold certainly can, and at various times *has*, gone up in value while other assets are going down. But the statistical relationship here is one that lacks correlation rather than one where the correlation is negative i.e. the assets move in *opposite* directions.

Aside from the qualitative benefits that gold offers – we drape it on our bodies to make ourselves appear attractive or convey our status – gold offers little else in terms of abstract or concrete utility. No earnings, no dividends, no compound interest. Quantitatively speaking, its lack of correlation with other assets classes might be the only characteristic of interest to investors. As a store of value it's only helpful over incredibly long windows of time.

Chapter 12.

IT'S NOT THE INFLATION HEDGE YOU THINK IT IS

"Gold will protect you from inflation!"

Raise your hand if you've heard this before. It's one of those things that everybody "knows" and accepts about gold. We hear it recited everywhere from industry analysts to talk-show hosts to advertisements on TV for gold dealing services.

Apparently, not enough people have looked at the actual data. When you study the historical price of gold, it becomes very clear very quickly that gold doesn't correlate very well with inflation at all. At least not over windows of several years. It doesn't today and it hasn't in the past.

Gold has collapsed during years when inflation was one of the highest rates on record. It has skyrocketed during periods in which there was hardly any inflation in sight. It's even gone *up* during rare environments of *deflation*[19].

Obviously, gold has correlated rather well with inflation over extremely long windows of time. We spent the previous section proving this point. The problem is that investors typically don't have investment horizons that long. The bulk of investors, even those who consider themselves "long term" investors, use horizons of 3-5 years for most of the decisions we make. Over windows of 3-5 years, anything can happen with gold. Inflation can go one way while gold can go another.

The idea of thinking of gold as an inflation hedge may be true over the course of several decades. But thinking of gold as something that will protect you from inflation over 3 years or 5 – even 7 or 10 years, is incorrect and can even be dangerous.

As an example, consider the period immediately after the bubble in 1981 and the low in 2001. Gold trended straight down, lower, and lower, and lower. Its price fell by over half. Yet those two decades were a period of unquestionably positive, albeit modest, inflation. The price level more than doubled. If an investor bought gold in the early 80's to hedge against future inflation – a time when everybody was in a frenzy to do so – the inflation hedge failed spectacularly for the next twenty years. Even someone who avoided the worst of the bubble and waited several years after the peak before buying this so-called inflation hedge, still wound up disappointed as gold kept falling in value while inflation steadily rose.

---

[19] The price of gold gained 11.8% between August 2008 and January 2009, a period where the Consumer Price Index (CPI) fell 3.5%.

Eventually gold caught back up during the post-2001 bull market. But it had taken nearly 30 years to finally act as an inflation hedge. And after the decade of the 70's where inflation was averaging between 7 and 11% per year, the early 1980's were a time when the need for an inflation hedge was most demanded. The moment when the world most wanted protection against inflation was the beginning of an era where gold would fail spectacularly to do it.

Gold also fails as an inflation hedge over much shorter windows of time such a single year. Let's consider some data.

TABLE 1 CHANGE IN GOLD PRICE VS. INFLATION RATE[20]

Year	Change in inflation rate (CPI)	Change in gold price
2013	1.5%	-27.3%
2012	1.7%	8.2%
2011	3.0%	11.6%
2010	1.1%	29.2%
2009	2.7%	25.0%
2008	0.1%	4.0%
2007	4.1%	31.6%
2006	2.5%	23.9%
2005	3.4%	17.8%
2004	3.3%	4.4%
2003	1.9%	21.7%
2002	2.4%	24.0%
2001	1.6%	1.4%
2000	3.4%	-6.1%
1999	2.7%	1.0%
1998	1.6%	-0.6%
1997	1.7%	-21.7%
1996	3.3%	-4.6%
1995	2.5%	1.2%
1994	2.7%	-2.0%
1993	2.7%	17.5%
1992	2.9%	-6.0%
1991	3.1%	-8.5%
1990	6.1%	-3.7%

[20] Source: Bureau of Labor Statistics

It's Not the Inflation Hedge You Think It Is

1989	4.6%	-2.3%
1988	4.4%	-15.3%
1987	4.4%	24.5%
1986	1.1%	19.0%
1985	3.8%	6.0%
1984	3.9%	-19.2%
1983	3.8%	-14.8%
1982	3.8%	12.0%
1981	8.9%	-32.1%
1980	12.5%	12.0%
1979	13.3%	132.6%
1978	9.0%	37.1%
1977	6.7%	22.7%
1976	4.9%	-4.3%
1975	6.9%	-27.1%
1974	12.3%	72.7%

Gold has *fallen* in value in 16 of the last 40 years, years in which there was *positive* inflation.

The correlation coefficient – which is how statisticians mathematically describe the strength of the relationship between two independent variables – between gold and the consumer price index is 0.47. For a data set of that size, that's not statistically meaningful. It's hardly a strong enough relationship to count on. Yet gold is regularly advertised as an inflation hedge, offering protection against the risk that the paper currencies in which it is denominated will erode in value.

The reason this myth persists is probably because gold has indeed acted as an inflation hedge over extremely long windows of time. But in a practical sense, gold is almost useless in this sense as there's a meaningful mismatch between a term of multiple-decades and terms that are more relevant for real-world investors. Investors who put gold bars instead of paper dollars under their mattress a century ago are in substantially better shape today. Over the last century, gold's price has risen tremendously while the purchasing power of $1 has declined with similar magnitude. In the 80s & 90s or the post-2011 years, however, the opposite has been true.

Gold is far from the only market in which investors make short-term decisions based on extremely long term patterns. It's damaging nonetheless, both in a psychological sense as our expectations from year to year fail to be met and in a fiscal sense as our investments yield different or disappointing results.

Gold also isn't the only asset that acts as an inflation hedge over the long run. Yet for some reason, it's the one that's most closely associated with it. A lot of assets have gone up in price over the last century and have thus have correlated positively with inflation. In fact, over the long, *long* run, virtually everything denominated in dollars goes up in price as the value of the dollars in which they're denominated falls. Real estate, art, a barrel of oil, stocks, or rights to the Beatles catalog. Most assets with the capacity to store value do it just as effectively as gold. Gold may have provided a very good big picture hedge against inflation during the 20th century, but plenty of other dollar-denominated assets did too. Not only is gold a statistically terrible hedge against inflation over the short run, over the long run, gold doesn't do it demonstrably better than real estate or stocks or other physical assets.

It's Not the Inflation Hedge You Think It Is

Gold also has a reputation for being forward looking. Some investors use it to try to divine future inflation. They'll point to action in the gold market and claim that it's telling a particular story about the future. Usually it's when prices are going up; one might hear that gold is rising because inflation will be higher in the future. As with any dramatic headline, it's important to dig a little deeper and separate fact from fiction.

Figure 4.1 looks a little confusing at first but it really isn't so bad. All it does is relate the *previous* 12 month change in the price of gold to the *subsequent* 12 month change in the inflation rate (as measured by the CPI). Since we were on some form of gold standard prior to 1974, it makes sense to only use data from that point to the present.

In a way, this chart is like climbing into a time machine and travelling backwards one month at a time. Each month the time machine stops and measures how far the gold price has risen in the last year and, since the time machine is from the future, compares it to how large the inflation rate actually wound up being in the coming year. Each dot represents one month – one stop in the time machine – and it measures the *prior year's* change in the gold price versus the *next year's* change in inflation.

Now we are officially ready to ask: does movement in the gold price predict future inflation?

FIGURE 4.2 CHANGE IN GOLD PRICE VS. FUTURE INFLATION (1 YEAR)

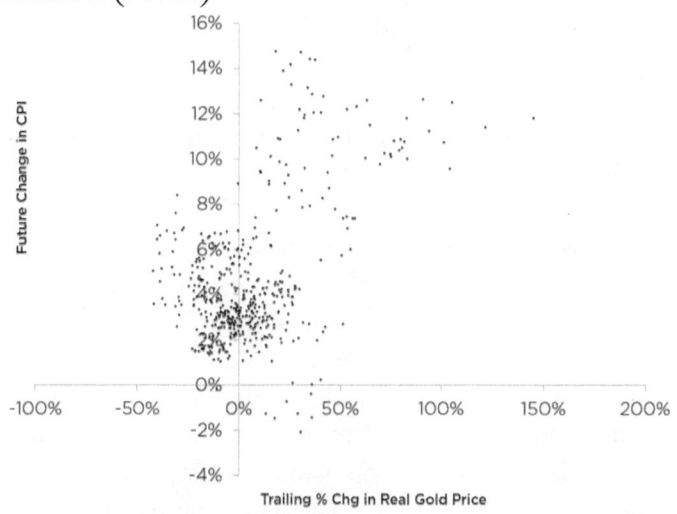

The answer is: sort of.

The slope of a regression line is clearly positive ($r^2 = 0.24$). That's just a fancy way of saying that there is indeed a positive correlation between past movements in gold and future movements in inflation. But the relationship is weak. Weak enough to not matter very much.

On top of that, there's a heavy skew between different types of environments. During normal times i.e. years with annual inflation between zero and 5%, gold does a very poor job predicting the future rate of inflation. Statistically speaking, it can't predict it at all. In plain English this means that just because gold prices go up, it doesn't mean above-average inflation will follow.

This could be because normal times are boring. Nobody really cares about inflation when it's in the low single digits. That's the official policy mandate, after all.

It's Not the Inflation Hedge You Think It Is

The Federal Reserve has two primary objectives, one of which is "price stability." Central bankers around the world sleep soundly and have happy dreams if inflation is positive and low.

So if the gold price is useless as an indicator during normal times, perhaps it can predict extreme times. Can gold predict when *hyper*inflation is on the horizon?

In the scatter chart you can see that when gold has really gone wild, increasing by 50% or more over a twelve month span, it has usually meant that a very high rate of inflation has followed in the coming year. This a very small data set, though. The U.S. has only had one bout with extreme inflation in the modern era. All of these data points are from the late 70's and early 80's. At that point the gold market was held in the grips of a speculative frenzy and the country had already been experiencing extremely high inflation for years. In practice, none of those data points would have been particularly useful.

The take-home point here is that one should be careful when trying to use the gold market to divine the future. Obviously, investors should always be careful about using special indicators to predict the future. But gold is a case worth emphasizing.

Gold is only effective as a very long term hedge against inflation and over the short run it can be a downright-terrible hedge against inflation. On top of that its price action also offers very little predictive value.

Chapter 13.

GOLD ISN'T MONEY

One of the most common characteristics cited of gold by those with the most faith in its religion is that gold is "real money."

"Money," by definition, is a medium of exchange that is legally recognized by a sovereign entity. It is, by definition, something that can be easily exchanged for a good or service. When you walk into a store to purchase a carton of milk, it is not only legal to trade dollars for the good, it is easy and commonly accepted.

As an experiment for whether or not gold effectively acts as money, try buying a TV from your local electronics retailer with an ounce of gold. Or try buying a new car with a stack of shiny gold coins. Not only does the government not recognize gold as a legal medium of exchange, in practice, neither do any of our economy's participants.

Money must also act as a unit of account or a method of measurement. Gold fails this test as well. We measure everything in the U.S. economy in terms of Dollars, not ounces of gold. The same is true regardless of which country you visit in the world. Every economy uses its own currency or the currency of another nation as a unit of account. Gold is not how we measure things.

Lastly, for something to be recognized as money, it must act as a store of value. For an economy to function successfully, its constituent bodies must have a place where they can accumulate wealth and store their savings, the quantitative result of all their work.

Over very long windows of time, gold passes this test with flying colors. It's an excellent store of value for someone with a 50 or 100 year horizon. But over shorter windows of time, windows which are far more relevant for consumers and savers in an economy, gold fails this test spectacularly. From month to month, gold is a wildly volatile asset class. We'll address this volatility in more detail in the next chapter, as the concept is tremendously important in other ways. For this section, suffice it to say that in order for something to act as money, it needs to preserve its value from month to month and year to year. It needs to instill confidence that when one receives it in exchange for goods and services, one will be able to turn around and exchange it for new goods and services of similar value. Gold does not do this.

As it happens, not even all paper currencies do a good job storing value. The world's major currencies – The Dollar, The Yen, The Euro, The Pound Sterling, The Renminbi, The Won – all excel at storing value, especially within their own economies. But lesser currencies, especially those that aren't pegged to one of the world's major currencies, can and do fail to act as stores of value over short windows of time. Zimbabwean Dollars obviously weren't a very good store of value. However, all one needs to do is take a closer look at these economies with shaky currencies. Inside them, consumers and savers seek the safety of major currencies wherever they can. Dollars, Euros, and the like are widely accepted, and in many cases, *preferred*, in the world's undeveloped economies.

Now, gold certainly does have a long history of being used as money. In fact, for the overwhelming portion of its history individuals in cultures both advanced and primitive have been exchanging gold as payment for goods and services. As recently as 200 years ago in the United States, gold was recognized as money. One could walk into a trading post and purchase a pick axe with gold coins.

But the 21st Century United States isn't Ancient Sumer, nor is it even the post-Revolutionary emerging economy that it once was. It's been almost a century since the world ceased making coins as currency. It's been even longer since any developed nation used them as a primary method of monetary exchange. None of that will be changing any time soon.

Even though gold shouldn't be considered real money, it can, however, be thought of as something of a "neutral currency."

The most important thing to understand about currencies is that they are all *relative value* propositions. Currencies don't have an independent, absolute value the way other assets do. Instead they are globally priced in terms of other currencies. The value of a British Pound is different depending on whether you are using U.S. Dollars, or Japanese Yen, or Euros to price it.

Currencies can even be priced in terms of other assets, which can be a little counter-intuitive. Last Halloween I went to the grocery store and there was a big box of pumpkins outside. Thanks to a confusing typo, it seemed that the grocery store was strangely pricing *dollars* in terms of pumpkins. The sign read:

$1 / 4lbs pumpkin

The sign should have read "Pumpkins: $0.25/lb." That's the way we typically think of produce or meat – dollars per pound – at the grocery store. As an economist, I was amused by flipping the relationship and determining that one dollar was actually worth 4 pounds of pumpkins. In this strange pumpkin-based economy, I'm sure you're wondering how many pounds of pumpkins an ounce of gold costs? About 5,000 pounds of pumpkin[21]!

I concede that economists have a strange sense of humor. But by pricing one thing in terms of another thing, we can better understand the way that gold and other currencies actually work. In the currency world, everything is relative. Given the way that gold behaves over long windows of time – a near-perfect hedge against the declining value of the paper currencies in which it is denominated – gold can act as an interesting "neutral currency" by itself.

The point is that when viewed on the global level, these relative-value relationships can change quickly and dramatically. It takes time for Americans to feel or even notice the erosion in value of the U.S. Dollar. But when

---

[21] As of 12/31/2013

both the numerator currency *and* the denominator currency are allowed to fluctuate, we can see a very different sense of how currencies change value.

Here's an example:

In the summer of 2001 I went backpacking through central Europe, pretty much at the exact peak of the U.S. Dollar relative to other global currencies, and, for what it's worth, gold as well. At the time I was astonished at how cheap everything was over there. Hostels in Germany and Austria were only $5-10 dollars per night, while a bed & breakfast in Venice where I had the extravagant luxury of my own bedroom and a private bath cost me just $60. Greece was so cheap it bordered on being free. Less than $50 got me enough Drachmas to stay for several days and enjoy some of the most wonderful food I'd ever eaten. Even as a flat-broke college grad I felt like King Agamemnon!

I returned to Europe in the summer of 2007. It wasn't quite the low in the US Dollar relative to the Euro, but it was pretty close. Needless to say, the experience was substantially more expensive. A similar bed & breakfast in Venice cost well over twice as much. On our first night in town, my wife and I sought some pizza. We found some by the Rialto Bridge and it was substantially more expensive than I remembered from 2001 (though tasted every bit as good). On this trip, my dollars didn't take me nearly as far. Fortunately, since I'd had a few years of gainful employment, I had a bit more of them to offset their loss in global purchasing power.

Those two trips highlighted both aspects of what drives a currency's value. Between 2001 and 2007, the value of the U.S. Dollar fell over 30% relative to the Euro. At the same time, the value of the Dollar and Euro each also fell relative to a fixed basket of goods and services such as a slice of pizza and a night at a hotel. The result was paying roughly twice as much for the same things.

Unless you traveled beyond US borders, you probably haven't noticed such drastic changes in your own purchasing power. Most people don't have a very good sense of how valuable the dollars we hold in our bank accounts are relative to other currencies and assets. We slowly, eventually notice that it takes more of our Dollars to buy the same things than it did ten or twenty years ago. Over short windows of time, the relative value of currencies – the pricing of one currency in terms of another – is much more volatile, and depending on where you may be traveling and spending your money, a much more visceral experience as well.

It helps to think of gold in this way. Gold performed very well between 2001 and 2009 in U.S. Dollar terms, gaining roughly 300%. But if you were a Venetian who had purchased gold denominated in Euros, your gain was only 156% over that same window. This matters.

Since gold is globally priced in dollars, gold is very dependent on the relative value of those dollars. If you're purchasing gold from another country, you must first convert your local currency to Dollars before making the purchase. That relationship can change a great deal from month to month or year to year. Meanwhile, the future price of the gold you purchase is inextricably linked to the fate of the paper currency in which you've purchased it. Dollar-denominated gold will perform much better when the US Dollar is under substantial pressure. Dollar strength typically tends to be a fairly large headwind for gold.

The Religion of Gold

It takes a bit of mental gymnastics, but by thinking of gold not concretely as "real money" and instead abstractly as a "neutral currency," it can help us spot opportunities we'd otherwise miss and avoid traps we'd otherwise stumble into.

Don't make the mistake of thinking gold is money. It isn't.

Chapter 14.

GOLD IS NOT A SAFE HAVEN

The definition of "safe haven" isn't just clear and straightforward. It's not subject to debate. There is one meaning and it is universally agreed upon.

A safe haven is an asset that can be relied upon to retain its value during periods of turbulence.

In the context of investments, a safe haven is one that can be expected to exhibit stability or even increase in price during moments of higher volatility. As an example, when stocks fall in value, investors tend to seek the safety that U.S. Treasuries or high quality bonds offer. When markets destabilize, investors become afraid and the way they make their fear go away is by shifting capital to investments that will retain their value.

These trends and behavioral patterns exist at the global economic level too. As the investments or currency of one country or region drop, individuals will reallocate their money to countries and regions perceived to be more stable. This "flight to safety" can take many forms.

Even at the local economic level, consumers and businesses will choose to save rather than spend or invest when they perceive the economy to weaken or the value of their assets and commodities to drop. In periods of economic instability, they'll seek the safe haven that Dollars offer. Dollars can be counted on to retain their value over short windows of time.

Stop me if you've heard the following headline before, which was actually excerpted from an actual article in a major national publication whose name will go unnoted:

Gold Gains On Safe-Haven Buying

```
Gold prices are moderately higher
in early U.S. trading Tuesday, as some
more safe-haven demand has surfaced
amid the simmering geopolitical situa-
tion...
```

It's unclear where this idea of gold as a safe haven originated. It's possible that this could be one of those qualities deeply embedded in and intrinsic to the religion of gold. For thousands of years, individuals have used gold in one way or another to either transact or to store value. It's strongly, and in an indirect way, correctly, related to our concept of currency. A portion of the population can still remember when our paper Dollars or our exchange rate were actually backed by gold bullion. Because of this history, we perceive safety in a place where it doesn't actually exist.

It's also possible that gold, by virtue of not correlating with risk assets like stocks will occasionally rise on a day when everything else is falling. Technically, there is no relationship between the price of gold and the price of the stock market on any given day or month. The monthly correlation between the two is 0.01, which is a statistical way of saying with nearly 100% confidence that how one asset moves has nothing to do with the other. Because these assets are completely unrelated in their performance, there will be some days or months where gold goes up while stocks go down. When that happens, it's much easier for the financial media to explain that gold is rising when stocks are falling because investors are "seeking a safe haven." Everyone is, of course, silent about the "safety" of gold during those days and months when stocks and gold both drop. That happens just as often.

We can actually break that pattern down even further and with even greater specificity. In the 468 months between 1975 and 2013, the stock market declined in 182 of them. Of those 182 months where the stock market dropped, gold *rose* in 99 and *fell* in 83 of them. It's not quite 50/50, but it's close. It's basically a coin toss whether investors will flee the risky stock market in any given month for the perceived safety of gold. And that's not what we would expect if gold were indeed a true safe haven, something that retained its value during moments of turbulence. In the real world, it only manages to do that about half the time.

Because of the way that information is disseminated in our culture and because of our deeply embedded historical biases, it's easy to perpetuate the notion that gold is a safe haven. It's a positive feedback loop. We hear someone say something that confirms our basic beliefs and those beliefs become slightly more entrenched. It doesn't matter if the belief is right or wrong. The belief exists, and so we look for patterns and behavior that confirm it, and when we see them, even if they are insufficient in number or strength, our beliefs harden. Because of this confirmation bias, it's easy for individuals to think that gold will retain its value during periods of volatility or instability.

Part of the problem is that over extremely long windows of time the data supports this idea of a safe haven. Gold does indeed act as a store of value, but only over periods of 30 or 50 or 100 years. It rises through the centuries roughly equivalent to the rate at which the paper currencies in which it is denominated fall. That's exactly what a store of value is supposed to do. We explored that in depth in Part 2.

The behavioral sin we frequently and regularly commit, however, is applying those extremely long-term qualities over shorter windows of time. In gold, these "short" windows can be as long as a decade or two. At the end of 1980, almost a year after the bubble popped, one needed to pay $589 for an ounce of gold. By the end of the year 2000, that ounce of gold was worth $273. Most individuals would agree that two decades is a long time. But it's not long-enough for whatever safety gold offers to actually come into play. Over that window, gold was an atrocious safe haven – at least as defined by the ability to retain its value. When adjusted for inflation, this failure was even more dramatic. In real terms, gold lost over 75% of its value between 1981 and 2001.

Most of the world would agree that safe havens aren't supposed to lose 75% of their inflation-adjusted value over a period of two decades. But this actually happened with gold. It wasn't even the first time it catastrophically failed to retain its value, either. Gold lost 46%

of its nominal value between the beginning of 1975 and August 1976. It lost nearly 40% of its nominal value between 2011 and the end of 2013. Rest assured, in the future this pattern will continue.

We can even quantify this failure to retain value with mathematical precision. Since gold could be owned freely by the public in 1975, gold's monthly standard deviation is 5.7%. Without getting too far out into the weeds of stochastic analysis, the standard deviation for a data set is simply a measure of how dispersed the data is from its average value. It's a way of quantifying volatility.

To see what that kind of volatility looks like visually, take a look at Figure 4.3. Each dot represents one month. This chart appears noisy, but it brings into focus the idea of how dramatically gold's value can change from month to month.

FIGURE 4.4 THE VOLATILITY OF GOLD

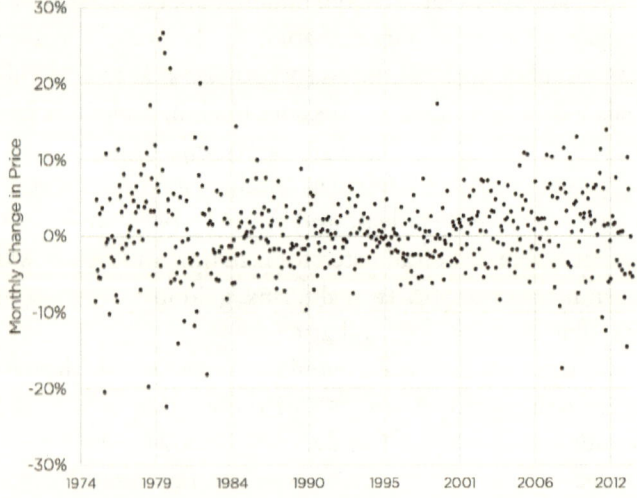

In annualized terms, gold's volatility is 19.6%. That tells us that in any given year the range of outcomes is huge. With an average annual return of 4.8% between 1975 and 2013 and a standard deviation of 19.6%, we would predict roughly one year out of three to be *outside* the already gigantic range of -14.8% and 24.4%.

Between 1975 and 2013 the returns for gold *actually were* outside that range 32.5% of the time. In the years ahead, this data is useful for framing our expectations.

Talk about volatility!

Is that what you are looking for in your safe haven?

If all this talk about statistics doesn't mean much to you, we can put this into context. The annualized volatility of the stock market over that same period of time was only 15.1%.

Stocks are less volatile than gold.

There is no debating this data.

No one in their right mind would suggest that the stock market is a safe haven. Every financial professional in the world will agree that of the major asset classes, stocks are the most volatile, the asset with the greatest risk. No one – least of all an investor on Main Street – believes that stocks should be counted on to preserve their value from month to month or year to year. Yet still, stocks do a better job of this than gold. And not just by a small margin, either. The difference between annualized volatility of 15.1% and 19.6% is meaningful.

Yet ironically, it is gold – one of the most volatile asset classes in the world – that has the reputation of being a safe haven.

For our penance, we must reject this notion that gold is a safe haven whenever we hear it. It simply isn't true. We must fall back on the data and remind ourselves that the conclusions we draw need to be evidence-based rather than narrative-driven. We should always question the teachings of our ancestors.

Outside the church of gold, in the world of real investors and real investing, this idea of gold as a safe haven is incredibly destructive. It causes tangible, concrete harm to investor portfolios. More insidiously, it causes widespread psychological discomfort. Investors who seek gold under the false notion that it's a safe haven are left either confused or angry after gold falls 5 or 10% in a given month or quarter, as it so frequently does. Those emotions can then catalyze a chain reaction of bad decisions, a Pandora's Box of potential losses throughout an investor's portfolio.

Chapter 15.

CASH HAS BEEN A BETTER INVESTMENT

Of all the realities central to gold, this is perhaps the most inconvenient.

We think of gold as an asset that's a virtual guarantee to protect us from the long, slow devaluation of the world's paper currencies. As evidenced in Part 2, over extremely long windows of time, that idea is even correct. But lost in that abstraction while singing the gospel of gold, we forget a crucial chunk of concrete reality: interest rates.

In the real world, people don't hold cash the way they do gold. They don't bury it in their back yard or lock it in a safe deposit box. They deposit their cash in a bank and receive interest in exchange. This interest is what offsets the purchasing power we lose every year from those dollars on deposit. Otherwise, why would we keep the dollars in the bank? Why wouldn't we invest them or spend them since, in an inflationary economy, those dollars are a guarantee to lose value?

Banks have been paying interest to depositors since the beginning of the banking industry. It's the fundamental dynamic linking lender and borrower.

In terms of purchasing power, the Dollar has lost roughly 96.7% of its value since the year 1900. This is a dramatic and oft-cited statistic, but the notion is even more impactful when considering specific examples.

A hundred years ago, $1,000 represented nearly an entire year's wages for many Americans. Today that same $1,000 pays for just a single month's mortgage or rent payment for a typical American. A hundred years from now, that same $1,000 will be worth even less. Assuming a similar rate of inflation over the next century to what we experienced during the last, $1,000 might only buy dinner for two at an average restaurant. (In this example, $1,000 a hundred years from now is worth roughly $45 today.)

I'll gladly pay you Tuesday for a hamburger today.

For millennia we have understood that "a dollar tomorrow is worth less than a dollar today." The way that we reconcile that is through interest rates. Interest rates ensure that we receive more dollars tomorrow if we lend them out to someone else, which includes depositing them in a bank. Interest rates are what help us offset that loss in purchasing power and decline in the value of each individual dollar.

Today, this carries an obvious and important caveat. The interest rates being paid right now on cash or low-risk debt are *less* than the rate of inflation. Even after that interest, the dollars on deposit in a bank still lose purchasing power every year. It's been this way for several years, too.

Even during the 1970's when inflation was rising at a double-digit pace, cash still paid 10-20%. U.S. Dollars became a whole lot less valuable through the 1970's, but the only way individuals actually felt that loss in purchasing power was if they were holding those dollars under their mattress or in a coffee can. Each dollar on its own may have been worth substantially less at the end of that wave of hyper-inflation, but thanks to interest rates, depositors had more of them to offset the loss.

Recently, however, this dynamic has broken down.

At the end of 2007, the Fed Funds rate – an overnight rate that banks charge each other and a common proxy for the yield on short-term, zero-risk investments – was 4.24%. People could deposit their money in a savings account and earn a rate of return that was slightly greater than the purchasing power their dollars lost due to inflation.

By August of 2008, the Fed Funds rate had dropped to 2%, just high enough to break savers even after inflation.

By December, the Federal Reserve dropped the Fed Funds rate to effectively 0%. Cash featured an inflation-adjusted yield on the order of *negative 2%*. One year prior, dollars on deposit were guaranteed to grow at a rate that offset the rate of inflation and provide a little extra return as a cushion. At the end of 2008, dollars on deposit represented a guaranteed way to lose wealth.

There are a lot of reasons why the Federal Reserve adjusts the Fed Funds rate. The primary objective is to stimulate the economy when it's in danger of slowing down. When interest rates, including the rates paid by banks in savings accounts, are low, it creates an incentive to borrow money and spend or invest.

As of this writing in 2014, both the Fed Funds rate and the average rate that banks pay on savings account are still effectively zero. In this environment, cash is guaranteed to lose value.

It's important to note, however, that this is a historical anomaly. Only during extreme environments has the short-term yield on cash dropped below the rate of inflation. For the last 60 years, the Fed Funds rate has averaged 5.2% per year. Over that same period, inflation has increased by an average of 3.7% per year.

The consequences of such a policy are beyond the scope of this book. It goes without saying that Federal Reserve policy during the 2008-2014 years has been one of the most intensely debated topics in modern history. We're in the middle innings of one of the biggest economic experiments in history. So far we've observed a recovery in U.S. economic growth. We've seen a re-inflation of risk assets. But it's still unclear exactly how much of that is attributable to the monetary climate. The second- and third-order effects of all this policy are still unknown.

There's little doubt that a decade or two from now, the market will still be debating exactly what all the effects were and whether they were worth it. The one thing we can all agree on however, is that this type of policy is extreme, and though it has persisted for nearly six years, it is by no means representative of the majority of U.S. economic history. For centuries, people have demanded a rate of return on their cash in order to preserve their purchasing power. In time, that will be the case again.

The Religion of Gold

✣

The slow, steady erosion of the value of paper currencies is one of the primary philosophical concepts that has fueled demand for gold over the decades. In certain pockets of the population, it has created an enthusiastic distrust for paper assets and ardent faith in the ability of gold to protect one from this inflationary devaluation.

It's not that this faith is misguided. To the contrary, over long windows of time gold does indeed protect one against progressively less powerful dollars. It's that, for some strange reason, interest rates are left out of the equation. This is where the data becomes quite strange, because cash + interest has delivered better performance than gold over the long run.

Figure 4.5 shows how cash (plus interest) has performed relative to gold. In this example, the interest rate we are using for cash is simply the Fed Funds rate.

FIGURE 4.6 CASH VS. GOLD

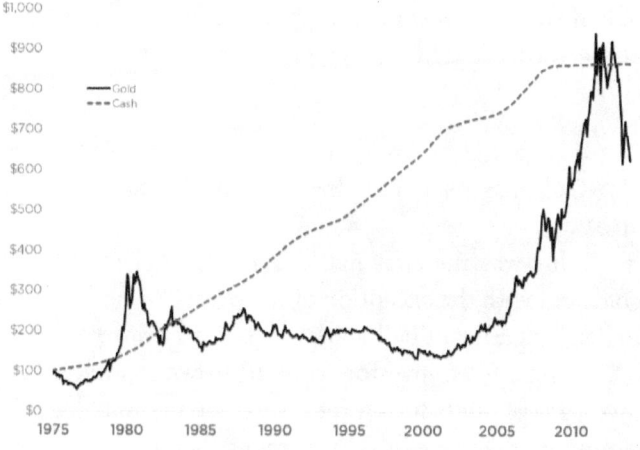

Obviously, that performance will differ depending on when you start your study. Here we use the beginning of 1975 as the starting point, as that was the first date in modern history where individuals could freely and legally own gold as an investment. If one selects a start date in 1980 or 1981, the outperformance of cash is even more dramatic. If one selects a start date in 2000 or 2001, gold has clearly been the superior performing asset.

This study can also look different depending on which interest rate we choose. The Fed Funds rate is an overnight rate that banks charge to each other. By its character, it is the lowest yielding and highest quality investment that can be had. It is the North Star upon which nearly every interest rate compass is fixed and influences the course that all assets chart. Alternatively, one could also use a rate such as the yield on 1-year Treasury Bills for this type of study. The results are very similar. Short-term Certificates of Deposit (CDs) and even the interest rate on a typical savings account tend to be higher than the Fed Funds rate at any given point in time. If we select one of these interest rates as the basis for our study, cash outperforms gold by an even greater amount.

Tangential to this is another uncomfortable reality:

Gold has really only been a good investment since 2001.

This was the first major, modern bull market for gold, and with the exception of the pre-1980 bubble, it's the only significant bull market in gold's history.

Before 1975, investors couldn't own it. And unless investors got out during the frenzy of the bubble, gold wound up being a worse investment than interest-yielding cash in the mid and late 70's. Even if you were somewhat fortunate in your timing, when adjusted for *risk*, cash was still arguably the superior investment during that rocky period. Once the bubble burst, gold was a bad investment through the entire 80's and 90's in absolute terms and disastrously bad investment after adjusting for inflation or related to any sort of cash-equivalent with a positive yield.

Only since 2001 has gold really been worth it.

This brings up an important point in the religion of gold. The gold narrative has totally changed. The way we think about gold today – the talking points, the passion, the ways we get exposure – is largely a modern convention. Much of what we hear circulated in the industry about the benefits of gold as an asset class is a retroactive re-writing of not just the last 50 years, but the last few thousand.

Interestingly enough, 1999-2001 was also the window when our basic gold model suggested that you should put the boat in the water and start loading it to the max. That was when gold was historically, massively undervalued. In most of our careers, those of us in the financial industry had never seen gold project to be as favorable a long-term investment as it was right then. It was one of the best moments to buy any asset at any point in history, and what followed was one of the greatest bull markets in the modern era.

I have little doubt that had I published such a study in 1999 and claimed that gold was a generational buy, it would receive just as much criticism as saying gold was a generational sell in 2011. Getting bullish about gold in the heat of the tech bubble was about the most contrarian thing an investor could do.

✠

The data behind these points this isn't subject to debate. Gold has had an uneven run since 1975 and cash has performed better. Over the long run, cash + interest isn't just a higher-returning "investment" than gold, it also does it with increased reliability and significantly lower volatility. Granted, the historically aberrant condition today whereby the yield on cash is virtually non-existent impacts our recent results and more importantly, influences our perception of cash-on-deposit as a competing store of value. When interest rates are zero and inflation is positive, gold can be a superior store of value to cash (and should be over sufficiently long windows of time).

It's also with a certain degree of faith that we say that, eventually, the artificially low interest rate environment of the post-crisis era will end. When the interest one receives on cash exceeds the rate of inflation, cash will return to the reliably superior investment over very long windows of time.

The more important point to remember is the general case. When thinking of gold and cash as competing assets, we frequently neglect to incorporate how interest rates influence that competition. We too often think of cash the same way we think of gold – as a pile of stuff sitting around in a safe deposit box. This is incorrect. Cash doesn't work this way.

In a positive-inflation vacuum, gold, as an asset denominated in dollars which steadily decrease in value over time, is incontrovertibly a superior investment to cash. But because of interest rates, a financial mechanism with a history nearly as ancient as gold, cash is a more robust and reliable store of value over periods both short and long.

Chapter 16.

WE'RE NEVER GOING BACK TO A GOLD STANDARD

The argument for a gold standard has a practical, and even desirable objective at its core. The goal is to preserve the value of the Dollar. Economies that sought out a gold standard with the primary objective of preserving price stability.

Implementing a gold standard in today's economy would be highly impractical for a number of reasons.

At the top of the list, there simply isn't enough gold to sustain today's global monetary system. There's only so much gold in the world and current quantities are insufficient to be able to provide appropriate backing for a major paper currency. Plus, the money supply needs to grow along with the economy. As a physical commodity with fixed supply and lumpy production, gold can hamstring an economy with its idiosyncratic supply & demand factors. A gold standard can be a concrete hindrance on an economy's ability to grow in accordance with its full potential. To keep up, increasing the supply of gold by aggressively boosting production is extremely expensive. Mining is a costly endeavor. There are more practical ways for an economy to allocate its resources than gold production in order to keep up with growth in the money supply.

On top of that, the logistics of large quantities of gold become challenging. It makes little sense for entities like central banks or large financial institutions to store gold in vaults given how expensive it is to store and secure. It's a layer of expense that public and private entities would rather avoid. Also, gold is physically cumbersome. Depending on the quantity, it can be nearly impossible to move if required.

A gold standard isn't just impractical for physical reasons. It makes little sense in the abstract either. Returning to a gold standard would eliminate the ability of the Federal Reserve or other global central banks to use monetary policy as a tool for stimulating or slowing the economy. A certain subset of the population would no doubt be excited by the prospect of the Fed losing its ability to influence markets and the economy. But there is substantial evidence to suggest that these modern monetary policy tools have tangible and quantifiable benefit.

Consider the Great Depression. While there were many factors that contributed to the U.S. recovery from that dramatic shock, it's almost universally accepted in the academic world that government intervention and monetary measures were among the most influential. Tightening monetary policy too quickly and curbing growth in the money supply in response to the recovery in 1934-1936 is believed to be the reason for the return to recession in 1937[22]. This high-profile policy blunder is as much evidence as one should need to be convinced that these types of monetary measures can indeed have a powerful effect on the economy. The effects don't have to be negative, though.

Virtually every major currency left the gold standard during the Great Depression. In fact, leaving the gold standard was a strong predictor of how severe and prolonged a country's depression wound up being[23]. Being on a gold standard eliminates a country's ability to expand the money supply to stimulate the economy. Nations that left the gold standard quickly such as Great Britain and Japan had quicker recoveries. Nations that remained on the gold standard for a few more years, such as the U.S., had larger downturns and recoveries that took longer. It wasn't until the Gold Reserve Act of 1934 and the adjustment of the gold-Dollar peg from $20.67 to $35/oz – a 40% devaluation of the Dollar and admission that the gold standard had failed at preserving price stability – that the economy finally began to heal. Consumer confidence returned. Deflation stopped immediately. GDP, which was -23% in 1932 and -4% in 1933, grew to +17% in 1934. Only during 1941-1944 did the U.S. have more economic growth than it did in the year immediately after it breached the principles originally set forth in the Gold Standard Act of 1900. Monetary policy, though

---

[22] Gauti B. Eggertsson, "Great Expectations and the End of the Depression," American Economic Review 98, No. 4 (Sep 2008): 1476–1516;

[23] Bernanke, Ben (March 2, 2004). "Remarks by Governor Ben S. Bernanke: Money, Gold and the Great Depression". At the H. Parker Willis Lecture in Economic Policy, Washington and Lee University, Lexington, Virginia.

highly controversial in the politics of today, has a legitimate track record of positively influencing the economy *in extremis*.

More recently, the severe recession that the U.S. experienced in 2008 and 2009 was mitigated to an impressive degree by the monetary (and fiscal) tools that were deployed during that time. Studies suggest that, were it not for the intervention by the U.S. Government and Federal Reserve, the "Great Recession" would have been startlingly worse. GDP would have been about 11.5% lower and payroll employment would be less by roughly 8.5 million jobs[24]. The nation would also have entered a period of significant and prolong *de*flation, not unlike the Great Depression eighty years earlier.

Had the U.S. been on a gold standard during such an event, the monetary stimulus toolkit would have been non-existent. The economy would have fallen further and faster without any support from the U.S. Government and the Federal Reserve.

And consider this thought experiment. With a Dollar formally pegged to gold, when the supply of gold becomes relatively scarce, the Treasury is forced to raise interest rates in order to curb demand for gold relative to Dollars. This must happen regardless of the state of the economy. Higher interest rates increase demand for Dollars, and in a situation where the demand for Dollars has to be increased, higher interest rates may be forced on an economy and system ill-prepared to deal with them. Imagine a scenario where gold production slowed or where demand for gold increased due to unpredictable idiosyncratic factors. Imagine if at that same time the economy

---

[24] Alan S. Blinder and Mark Zandi, "How the Great Recession Was Brought to an End", July 27, 2010

was also entering recession. What sort of effect might sharply higher rates have at the onset of recession? How might individuals change their consumption and investment patterns if, just as their confidence was beginning to erode, it suddenly became more difficult to access credit or if they were given a stronger incentive to keep more dollars on deposit with their bank rather than spend or invest them? The potential outcomes range from painful to catastrophic.

When the U.S. was on a gold standard, the economy was subject to frequent cyclical oscillations. Since abandoning the gold standard the business cycle has smoothed considerably and recessions are both less common and less severe.

Between the years of 1900 and 1934 when the U.S. was on a formal gold standard, the economy suffered 10 recessions with an average peak-to-trough decline in business activity of -23%. In the 80 years since, the U.S. has experienced just 13 recessions. The average drop in GDP has been slightly worse than -4%. Since abolishing the "gold exchange standard" in 1974, the economy has experienced only 5 recessions with an average drop in GDP of merely -2.2%. That includes the "Great Recession" of 2008 & 2009, as well as the twin recessions of 1980 and 1981-1982, all of which are commonly considered to have been significant. A drop in output or business activity of 10-20% may seem unfathomable today; during the era of the gold standard, it was quite common. It wasn't merely correlation, either. Recessions are less painful in the era of modern central banking because we have far more tools to fight them than we did under a gold standard.

Even if there were no such need for monetary policy to stimulate a slow economy or cool one flirting with too much growth or inflation, gold standards do a remarkably poor job at their original objective: price stability. Gold is a tremendously volatile commodity. With gold backing the currency, the price level in the economy becomes subject to wild fluctuation. Changes in supply and demand for gold have systemic economic impact.

A volatile price level is exactly what we saw during the years the U.S. was on a formal gold standard. The period between 1900 and 1934 featured both the highest and the lowest peaks in the inflation rate. The U.S. flirted with deflation briefly in the middle of the last century, but by and large, deflation was a phenomenon unique to the era of the gold standard.

FIGURE 4.7 ANNUAL % CHANGE IN THE CPI

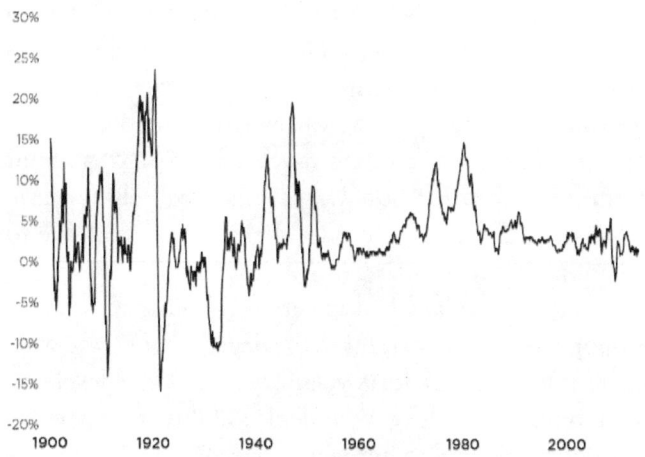

The data is as clear as it gets. Prices were far less stable during the era of the gold standard.

Consumers today complain about modest, positive inflation. Can you imagine how they might respond with changes in the price level of 15% or more? Or periodic deflation of 10-15%?

Over the long run, gold is indeed a stable store of value. Over very long periods of time, backing a currency with gold should preserve price stability. But over short windows of time, even windows as long as ten or fifteen years, this functionality disintegrates completely. After 114 years, we have sufficient data to be convinced of this.

Finally, there's simply no need to back a paper currency with an asset like gold that has intrinsic value. A U.S. Dollar may only have value because we all agree it has value. But one can and will always be able to use paper Dollars to settle one's debts with the government i.e. pay taxes. As long as individuals have a need to pay taxes and the government will accept them as such, paper Dollars will always have intrinsic value. You and I will always need them and can therefore feel confident using them to transact goods and services. The government rejecting its own currency or eliminating the taxes it levies on its citizens are events to which we can assign low enough probabilities that it isn't worth much time worrying about them. Like them or not, U.S. Dollars will always have value, even if that value erodes slightly every year due to inflationary forces.

A gold standard makes very little sense in today's economy. It's only helpful to the degree that we are willing to tolerate short-term volatility in the price level and wish to take away the government's ability to use monetary policy as a tool to influence the economy. It impedes growth at our full economic potential and introduces numerous abstract and concrete challenges. Calling for a return to a gold standard requires ignoring crucial economic evidence, adhering instead to cult-like religious faith. Individuals promoting these beliefs should be regarded with skepticism and a critical eye.

Chapter 17.

EVERY INVESTOR SHOULD OWN GOLD

As an asset class, gold has myriad flaws. It doesn't do anything. It's a poor short- and medium-term hedge against inflation. Nobody uses it as money. It has extreme price volatility and fails dramatically as a store of value. It's nowhere close to a safe haven. And over the long run, it appreciates in value at a slower rate than cash + interest.

That said, there is unquestionable benefit for owning a little bit of gold in one's investment portfolio.

Much of this book has been devoted to debunking gold-related myths and dispelling wrongly-held beliefs. The religion of gold requires blind faith. But by opening one's eyes to data and perspectives that are based on tangible evidence, gold takes on a different character. We see through its luster and avoid being hypnotized by the narratives of its history. Its color changes. It isn't a strictly negative change, either. To the contrary, gold can be a fantastically useful tool for investors.

If you've ever met with a financial advisor, you've surely heard something about building a "balanced portfolio." Diversification is one of the core principles that every financial advisor agrees on. Depending on one's age and risk tolerance, a diversified portfolio may contain something like 60% stocks and 40% bonds. If it's more sophisticated, it may also include assets such as real estate, foreign currencies, commodities, and alternative strategies. For most retail investors, however, that level of diversification across multiple asset classes is rare.

The reasons for owning gold vary depending on its price and other market factors. There are many. Only one reason matters, though, and it transcends all market environments: gold is different and it moves in totally different ways from other investments.

Gold doesn't correlate with any major asset class. Investments that don't correlate – investments that do their own thing irrespective of movements in other assets – can be incredibly powerful tools. They can be used to suppress overall portfolio volatility and increase long-term risk-adjusted performance. The core principle of diversification is powered by a lack of co-movement between the assets held in one's portfolio. This uniqueness is where gold truly excels.

The exact amount of gold one should hold in their portfolio depends on a number of things. The most important factor, as with any asset, is how its expected returns compare with the expected returns of other assets in the portfolio. As demonstrated in Parts 2 and 3, gold's expected returns are largely a function of its current price and valuation. When gold's intrinsic valuation is expensive, one should hold less of it, or in the case of an easily-identifiable bubble such as 1980 and 2011, none at all.

The forward returns in those situations are typically low. When gold is cheap, one should buy more. The return frontier is considerably more favorable when starting from depressed valuations.

Regardless of the factors influencing the relative attractiveness of gold as an investment, for most investors it shouldn't ever represent much more than 5% in one's portfolio. Beyond that the effects of gold's volatility begin to have a more noticeable impact on the portfolio as a whole.

Conventional wisdom within the world of investors who use gold as a tool for portfolio diversification is that the preferred way to own gold is via the physical metal. Gold coins typically carry a premium over the spot commodity price, but they're relatively easy to purchase. For most investors, they're also easy enough to store in a safe or deposit box. As with most investments, the most prudent philosophy to use when investing in gold is adopting a long-term stance. Don't buy or sell gold based on how you think it will perform over the next few months or years. Gold's short-term price movement is impossible to predict. Own it based on what it's expected to do over 5-10 years or more. Match it with the duration or expected lifespan of your other investments.

For investors who wish to avoid the transaction costs and hassles associated with gold coins and bars, there are more modern alternatives. The easiest way to add gold to one's portfolio is with an exchange traded fund (ETF). There are several gold ETF's, but the biggest and most popular is the SPDR Gold Shares ETF (GLD).

The important thing to understand and look for with these exchange traded funds is that the funds themselves hold the actual metal. If you buy GLD, you're technically buying shares of a trust that holds a whole lot of physical bullion. Because of this GLD will move in almost perfect lockstep with the actual price of gold.

One can also invest in gold by proxy by investing in the equity of companies that produce it. Over longer windows of time the two tend to be linked. The monthly correlation between the change in the price of gold and the change in the price of the Market Vectors Gold Miners ETF (ticker: GDX), a diversified basket of large gold mining stocks, is quite high. The monthly r-squared between the two since 2006 is 0.65. That suggests that 65% of the change in the price of a diversified basket of gold stocks can be explained by changes in the price of gold. Given the nature of their businesses – digging up gold from the ground and selling it – that should hardly come as a shock.

It's the fact that gold miners are *businesses* that is most interesting. Unlike Warren Buffet's hypothetical, impotent cube of gold, a gold mining company isn't just a thing that sits there doing nothing while only increasing in value over hugely long windows of time at the rate of inflation. A gold mining company is an enterprise. It's managed by intelligent executives. It extracts consumer surplus from the public. It generates profits for its shareholders. Gold mining companies can pay dividends, too. Over time, they appreciate in value much more than does the price of the commodity in which they are engaged in producing.

Consider the difference between the long-term increase in the price of gold and Barrick Gold Corporation, the world's largest gold miner.

FIGURE 4.8 GOLD VS. BARRICK GOLD CORPORATION
INDEX = 100

Even after the disastrous, hair-raising drop from the frothy levels of 2011, Barrick Gold Corporation has still returned substantially more than gold over the last three decades. Since 1985, Barrick has returned nearly 8% per year to its shareholders. Gold appreciated at a rate just over 5% per year during that same window.

Gold mining stocks also enjoy some of the same diversification benefits that gold does. Since 2006, the correlation of the Market Vectors Gold Miners ETF with the S&P 500 has been almost non-existent. The monthly correlation coefficient is 0.22 and the r-squared is 0.046. Less than 5% of the movement in the price of a diversified basket of gold stocks can be explained by changes in the price of the entire stock market. Over longer windows of time, the correlation breaks down even further. The monthly correlation coefficient between Barrick Gold Corporation and the S&P 500 since 1985 is 0.15. The r-squared is 0.023. Virtually none of the movement in Barrick's stock price over any given month can be explained by movement in the broad stock market. A year like 2013 where Barrick *lost* 48% of its value while the stock market *gained* 30% is a fascinating and convincing anecdotal data point that gold stocks act independently from the market in a way that other companies don't.

In any case, this is all just a fancy way of saying that gold miners, as dividend-paying corporations with a profit motive, demonstrably outperform gold over the long run, all while enjoying the same diversification & lack-of-correlation benefits of gold. These can be powerful tools for either amateur investors or professional portfolio managers. Even if you're building a portfolio consisting strictly of stocks, adding a basket of gold miners to the mix is a statistically-proven way to increase the portfolio's diversification. Investors should obviously consult a financial professional before deciding whether and how much exposure is appropriate for them.

Finally, a less appreciated way to "invest" in gold is by buying jewelry. It is by no means the most efficient way to access it, and it's one of the least liquid forms of gold, but it's arguably the most fun. Your spouse will thank you for it, too. For plenty of investors, that's worth the cost!

When it comes to using gold jewelry as a proxy for a gold "investment", just make sure the jewelry is of good quality. As an investment, the more pure the gold, the better. Gold coins are typically 24 karat (99.99% pure), but that level of purity doesn't always make for the most practical article of jewelry. Jewelry needs to be strong and durable, qualities that pure gold most definitely lacks.

Typically, gold jewelry is alloyed with other metals to increase its toughness and hardness. 14 karat (58.5% pure) and 18 karat (75% pure) gold jewelry are far more popular. If you are going to explore gold jewelry as an "investment", it's important to pay attention to its purity.

In the appendix we'll address some other ways of investing in gold. Some of them are a bit more sophisticated and technical.

✠

I feel as though I need to make one final thing clear. It's subtle distinction, but when I say that every investor should own some gold, this is different than saying that gold is a good bet to go up in price. Based on the conclusions of Part 2 and 3, it's clear that gold is a low-probability bet to increase at a rate greater than the inflation rate over the next several years, perhaps even longer than that.

Why recommend an asset when its expected returns under a relatively robust model are so unfavorable? Because the future is impossible to predict. Markets do unexpected things for unexpected reasons. Models break down and fail over windows short and long. Investors deal with uncertain and changing information. None of us have a crystal ball.

Even more importantly, intelligent asset managers don't slavishly allocate only to the assets that they believe will have the highest returns. They assemble portfolios out of pieces that fit well together. They add bonds, not because bonds have lower returns than stocks over the long run, but because bonds are subject to an entirely different set of economic inputs that influence their performance. Bonds are different than stocks, and both tend to rise in price over the long run. Such is the case with gold and the stocks of the companies who mine it. They are especially powerful portfolio *tools*.

Five thousand years ago, gold's purpose was that of a *tool*.

Such is the case today. Don't ascribe additional magical or god-like qualities to gold beyond its utility as a tool.

Conclusion

Like any religion, the culture of gold and popular investment in it is one dominated by deeply-entrenched, sometimes-ancient ideas. There's not a whole lot of mind-changing when it comes to how gold should be viewed and how it should be utilized as a tool in one's portfolio. Investors develop their beliefs about it, and that's that.

Unfortunately, investing is an endeavor that demands intellectual flexibility. Mind-changing is a necessary element for investing success – perhaps the most necessary over the long run. Investors get it wrong as often as they get it right, and when they do get it wrong, they need to be quick to react and change their mind as the facts and data dictate. Wrongness in the context of investing isn't merely an abstract concept; wrongness equates to concrete losses. If you get it wrong, you lose actual dollars. If you don't quickly correct the beliefs that caused it, you'll lose more of them.

Losses are an unavoidable component of the endeavor. It's OK for investors to lose money. But the ultimate goal of investing is to keep these losses to a minimum relative to our gains. Deeply-entrenched ideas and an unwillingness to change them can get in the way of accomplishing that. Ultimately, anybody who wants to invest in gold in one form or another needs to make a decision about which objective is more important: profit-maximization or a keeping-of-the-faith. At least half of the time throughout history, those two concepts have been at odds.

The most devout keepers-of-the-faith may be small in number but they have the loudest voices. The ideas promulgated by these few – the Gold Bugs and the paper money skeptics – have penetrated far and wide into mainstream investment culture. These ideas have shaped everyone else's understanding of gold. In most cases, it's an incorrect understanding too. Many of these basic ideas are just plain wrong.

To wit, even investors who know very little about gold or investing are likely to think that gold is an effective inflation hedge, a safe haven, or that it functions as money. Gallup polls investors regularly about which asset class they view to be the best long-term investment. Even after three years of disastrous performance, 24% of investors in 2014 perceive gold to be the asset with the best long-term returns. This was second only to real estate, roughly equal to sentiment for stocks & mutual funds, and significantly higher than fixed income investments such as CDs or bonds. In 2011, before the bear market in gold began, 34% of the public viewed gold to be the best long-term investment and no other asset class was close.[25]

What's even more disturbing is that there's a correlation with income. The further down the income spectrum you look, the higher that preference for gold grows. 31% of those with an income less than $30,000 per year

---

[25] Gallup. *Americans Sold on Real Estate as Best Long-Term Investment.* http://www.gallup.com/poll/168554/americans-sold-real-estate-best-long-term-investment.aspx

view gold to be the best long-term investment[26]. Our perception about investments and investing is heavily influenced by the culture surrounding us. Faith-based ideas, especially those with easily digestible talking points like gold, spread like wildfire, especially among the poor and uneducated.

Our perception of gold matters. A significant number of people view it to be the *best* investment, and even those that don't at least view it as an asset with a positive real return. Or they accept it as an "inflation hedge" and "safe haven." Yet none of these things are true. As deeply-entrenched faith-based concepts, they're better at playing to our emotions and our desire for psychological shortcuts than they are passing tests of analytical rigor. Presenting a data-driven case and demanding that listeners think critically is difficult. Most investors don't do this.

Obviously, the parallels between devout gold culture and the subject of religion are light and true only in the most general, big-picture sense. Gold *isn't* truly a religion, of course. But it's a place where unchecked fundamentalism can cause concrete harm, that is to say: losses.

In the world of investing, fundamentalism is as sure a bet for financial ruin as any. The financial markets are mercurial entities and have a knack for doing things and winding up at outcomes that we least expect. Not only do the markets demand continual alacrity from its participants, but they require that we occasionally do things that run counter to our originally held beliefs. With gold, those beliefs can run a little deeper and are linked to concepts that are more ancient than the beliefs surrounding

---

[26] Ibid.

Microsoft stock, the S&P 500, or the US Treasury market. With gold, it's harder to admit that our ideas are wrong.

When we get down to it, only two things matter as an investor: making more money and doing it with less risk. Neither is possible without a proper understanding of how the investment itself actually works.

Given the degree of misunderstanding about gold and our willingness to keep circulating incorrect beliefs – even among more sophisticated investors or in the financial media – it's clear we still have a long way to go.

Conclusion

Appendix:

Alternative Gold Strategies

Building a Practical, Simple Strategy for Gold

Now that all the basic points have been established, we can get a little more technical and put our new understanding to use. We can design some strategies that may seem slightly arcane to the layman but are demonstrably superior to simply buying and holding gold. They incorporate the lessons and history of the previous chapters and add a few new elements from professionals within the industry.

It's worth reiterating that the idea of having gold play some sort of role in an investor's portfolio is a modern convention. We all loved gold for a spell during the late 1970's. But two decades of declining price turned that love to hatred, or in most cases, apathy. It wasn't until the post-crisis years where the world started paying attention again and re-writing the history of our perception. Prior to around 2008, very few investors had any sort of gold strategy at all. It was mostly relegated to gold bugs and alternative asset managers. By 2010 it was a daily topic on CNBC. And suddenly the narrative was that we had loved and appreciated gold all along, entranced by its ancient history and unique investment qualities.

If we accept the principle underlying the model we discussed in Part 2, one in which the price of gold is related to and ultimately driven by the long-term trend of global inflation, then we can identify the moments in which gold is abnormally cheap or abnormally expensive. Even though that model is highly inaccurate in terms of exactitude, it does excel at pointing out the general locations when gold is *in extremis*. We can use this. For long-term investors who accept the idea that perfect timing is impossible, general locations are good enough. Our basic model also excels at providing context and understanding the type of background present in the market at any given point in time.

With this knowledge, we can design our first strategy, which is by no means optimal. It's just a very simple strategy that keeps you long gold for most of the time and gets you out during the rare moments when gold gets historically expensive. It takes you in and out somewhat slowly, too.

This strategy and all the ones that follow will begin in 1975. Prior to that year it was illegal to own gold as an investment and the price was artificially suppressed under different versions of the U.S. gold standard.

"4-Bucket" Strategy

Rules & Description:

- Split portfolio into four equal-sized buckets. Eg. $25,000 for a $100,000 portfolio
- In January (or any other arbitrary date) of each year, consult the gold price model.
- If the long-term projected return at that moment is greater than zero, that bucket buys gold or holds gold if it's already long[27].
- In the second January, the second bucket does the same thing, buying/holding if the model suggests positive long-term returns and selling/avoiding if the model suggests negative long-term returns.
- This continues until the fifth January when the first bucket makes another decision about whether to buy/hold or sell/avoid.

---

[27] Being "long" an asset means to own it with the hope or expectation that the price will rise. Being "short" implies having sold the asset short with the expectation of generating a profit if the price drops.

FIGURE 0.1 "4-BUCKET STRATEGY" PERFORMANCE

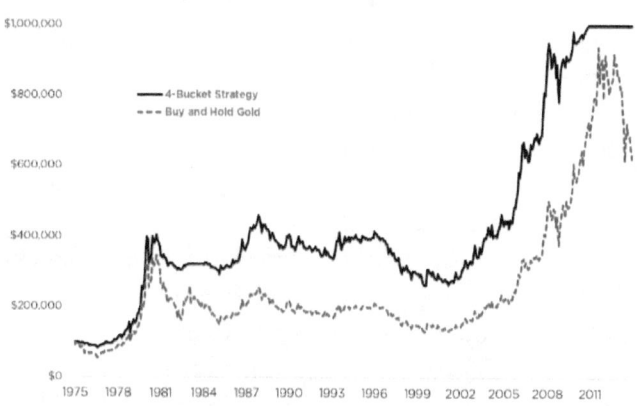

Strategy Performance:
Average Annual Return: 6.08%/yr
Annualized volatility: 14.39%

Buy-and-Hold Performance:
Average Annual Return: 4.81%/yr
Annualized volatility: 19.86%

As you can see, this strategy is a noticeable improvement on buying and holding gold. It lowers risk and helps investors avoid major bear markets such as those in the early 1980s and 2011-2013. Its approach is hardly perfect and both naïve and simplistic, but the real purpose of introducing such a strategy is to illustrate how easy it is to improve on buying and holding gold.

This is a very slow moving strategy, only making one change per year and in only one-fourth of the portfolio. For most of the time you're married to gold and its rocky ride. When prices get historically expensive, the strategy slowly scales you out. As they return to normal, the strategy slowly scales you back in. The underlying objective is basically to avoid bubbles and participate in cyclical bull markets.

I can already hear your first objection, and it's "if we knew where the bubbles were when we were actually in them, of course we'd get out!"

This is precisely the point. We do know when gold is in a bubble. That's the point of the models we outlined in Parts 2 and 3. As long as we define "bubble" more broadly as being a condition where prices are extremely, abnormally expensive relative to their long-term trend. In fact, being able to identify those moments of extreme overvaluation is arguably the only thing our model is any good at.

Even though our strategy is demonstrably more effective than buying and holding gold, there is a long list of things wrong with and an equally long list of ways that one could optimize it. Philosophically, though, the core idea – that we should own gold when it is cheap or fairly priced and avoid it when it is historically expensive – is a good one.

A four-year rotation strategy is certainly long enough in practice for most investors. Pragmatically, it works rather well. There's a foundational flaw, however, and it's that we are using a 10-year projection of returns to make a decision about a 4-year window of holding. The approach still works because when gold prices get historically expensive i.e. the implied future returns are negative, it usually winds up being both a poor long-term and medium-term investment. We can do better, however, by matching our 10-year holding period to our 10-year projection period.

Our next strategy is a "10-Bucket" super long-term strategy. What it lacks in practicality, it makes up for in philosophical rigor. We also introduce cash to our strategy. Funds that are not invested in gold are instead invested in a risk-free assets that pay a yield similar to the Fed Funds rate such as a money-market fund or 1-year Treasury Notes. Investors could also use short-term TIPS for the inactive buckets if they were, *ahem*, especially concerned about inflation.

"10-Bucket" Strategy

Rules & Description:
- Split portfolio into ten equal-sized buckets. Eg. $10,000 for a $100,000 portfolio
- In January (or any other arbitrary date) of each year, consult the gold price model.
- If the long-term projected return at that moment is greater than zero, that bucket buys gold or holds gold if it's already long[28].
- In the second January, the second bucket does the same thing, buying/holding if the model suggests positive long-term returns and selling/avoiding if the model suggests negative long-term returns.
- This continues until the fifth January when the first bucket makes another decision about whether to buy/hold or sell/avoid.

---

[28] Being "long" an asset means to own it with the hope or expectation that the price will rise. Being "short" implies having sold the asset short with the expectation of generating a profit if the price drops.

FIGURE 0.2 "10-Bucket Strategy" Performance

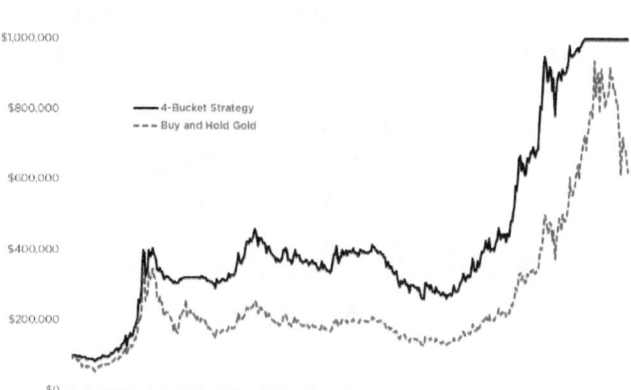

Strategy Performance:
Average Annual Return: 7.00%/yr
Annualized volatility: 13.03%

Buy-and-Hold Performance:
Average Annual Return: 4.81%/yr
Annualized volatility: 19.86%

This is a meaningful improvement on our original approach. It reduces our volatility from simply buying and holding gold by a third and adds an extra 2% per year over the long run. In risk-adjusted terms, this type of strategy is dramatically superior to owning gold outright.

$100,000 invested under this type of strategy in 1975 would have grown to $1.4 million by today, more than double the $624,000 you would have made simply by buying and holding gold the entire time.

Avoiding gold when it's historically expensive is the primary driver of the better performance in this strategy. A lot also has to do with putting our cash to work while it's idle. In the real-world, investors could improve on these returns even further by utilizing investments with longer durations such as a *10-year* Treasury Note (or TIPS) rather than a 1-year Note.

Because this strategy moves so slowly with its 10yr window and rotational approach, we never really get all the way out. It's extremely rare for gold to remain over-priced relative to trend for 10 consecutive years. In fact, this has never happened, and even at the beginning of 2014, this strategy would still be 30% long. This super-long-term approach may work well for investors who always want to have a little bit of exposure to gold but need some sort of guidance about how much exposure they should have.

Again, there are all sorts of ways you can tweak a strategy like this. You can use a different number of buckets, you can use a 7 year projection window, you can adjust your holding periods, you can rebalance more frequently, you can even change what the "idle" portion of the portfolio is invested in.

The strategic point is that when gold gets cheap, you should own more of it and when it gets expensive you should own less. I keep repeating this point and I realize it sounds obvious, but most investors really, truly, honestly do not act that way.

It's possible that you may reject the idea that gold should be avoided as a long-term holding when it's overpriced relative to trend. Or it's possible that you may have a shorter investment horizon. After all, just because gold is historically expensive doesn't mean it can't keep going up in price. This happens frequently throughout history in plenty other markets aside from just gold.

By shortening our perspective and modifying our core principal, we can design a different menu of strategies: trend-following.

Rather than messing around with trying to answer the question of whether gold is expensive or cheap, we can simply follow basic price action. When the trend is good, we own gold. And when the trend is bad, we avoid it and go to cash, Treasuries, or short-term TIPS[29] if inflation is a worry. Professional traders in the commodities futures industry have been employing these types of strategies for decades. They're still popular today and are among one of the few basic classes of strategy that have been proven to work over long windows of time.

---

[29] Remember: TIPS are Treasury *Inflation Protected* Securities. They are designed to adjust their principal higher or lower based on changes in the official inflation rate. They are in practice and theory a perfect hedge against inflation.

Basic Trend Following Strategy

Rules & Description:
- When gold's price is above its 12 month moving average, own gold.
- On a monthly close below the 12 month moving average, sell gold and go to cash or Treasuries.

FIGURE 0.3 BASIC TREND FOLLOWING STRATEGY PERFORMANCE

Strategy Performance:
Average Annual Return: 9.07%/yr
Annualized volatility: 15.25%

Buy-and-Hold Performance:
Average Annual Return: 4.81%/yr
Annualized volatility: 19.86%

You can see now why so many professional traders rely on basic strategies like this. In terms of total return, a trend-following strategy – even the most basic such as the one that this model employs – is dramatically superior. Buying and holding gold looks almost like a joke alongside this type of approach.

One of the problems with this strategy and the others mentioned so far is that short-term yields right now are close to zero. The Fed Funds rate is only slightly positive and yields on Treasuries are also historically low. When the portfolio or part of the portfolio moves to cash, it isn't appreciating in the way that it did in the 80's, 90's or 00's. With short-term yields below the inflation rate, our portfolio becomes a *negative real return* portfolio when it goes to cash.

Short-term yields won't stay this low forever, of course. But until they do, investors can explore alternative holdings to cash such as long-term TIPS or dividend paying stocks or other active-hedged strategies depending on their risk preference. Trend following strategies are extremely flexible and what one does with the assets when not following the trend is a matter of personal taste.

We can modify our basic trend following strategy in an interesting way, one that may especially appeal to investors who don't want to follow gold's price every day or month and instead want take a longer-term perspective.

Rather than being all-in or all-out as the previous strategy suggested, we can allow our portfolio to scale. Drawing from our first two "bucket strategies" we can split our trend following portfolio in two.

Lazy Trend Following Strategy

Rules & Description:
- Split portfolio into two buckets of 50% each.
- Every January, look at the current price of gold. If it's above the 12-month moving average, buy with one half of the portfolio.
- If the price of gold is below the 12-month moving average, sell that half of the portfolio or keep the portfolio in cash if already out.
- Every July, repeat the process with the other half of the portfolio.

FIGURE 0.4 Lazy Trend Following Strategy Performance

Strategy Performance:
Average Annual Return: 10.63%/yr
Annualized volatility: 15.30%

Under this approach, the portfolio has three possible states:
- 100% long – both buckets long
- 50% long – one bucket long
- 0% long – neither bucket long

The strategy makes a maximum of just two trades of year, and depending on the trend in January or July (or any other dates one chooses), the portfolio may not make any trades. It doesn't perfectly capture the spirit of trend following, but it replicates it easily enough for a lazy investor.

The performance of the lazy trend following approach is slightly better than the basic trend following approach. And the volatility is nearly identical. In practice and going forward, these two strategies will obviously vary in performance over short windows of time. Over longer windows, however, their performance will converge. Either is a clearly superior alternative.

This type of trend following approach may seem somewhat arbitrary, and it is. Investors can use different dates aside from January and July to do their rebalancing. They can use a 24-month moving average instead of a 12-month moving average as their signal. Or they can shorten their duration and use a 6-month moving average and four buckets instead of two. Or they can stick with just one bucket and use 10-month (200 day) moving average. The options are endless. Investors should find an approach that feels right, makes sense, and matches their level of activity. I've known professional traders who follow price trends of minutes or seconds and trade in and out of a market dozens of times per day.

The point is that nearly all of these trend-following approaches are superior to buying and holding gold over the long run. Investors should focus less on the exact details of how these strategies have performed historically, and instead select an approach that matches their personality, tolerance for volatility, and desired level of engagement.

✠

We can even blend the philosophies underpinning these two approaches – trend following and avoiding historical extremes – into a consolidated, more active strategy.

We can also kick it up a notch and incorporate leverage into our strategy. Really, all we're interested in is highlighting the impact of certain aspects of our trading models. Investors don't technically need to use it with these active variants, and obviously *shouldn't* if it isn't prudent given their financial situation. "Leverage" in this section can also be construed generally to mean "overweight" or "max-aggressiveness."

In any case, let's return to our simple 12-month trend following approach and add some valuation-based signals to enhance it. When gold gets historically cheap, the tailwinds of mean reversion start gathering and act has a performance-enhancer. Gold's performance is best when the trend is positive and when the valuation is also favorable. This is true for other asset classes as well, such as stocks. All markets tend to move in long cycles from moments of extreme undervaluation to moments of extreme overvaluation. The bull markets of the 1950s and 1980s (and even the post crisis bull market of 2009-to-day) ran so impressively and for so long because once positive momentum had been established, the market had a long way to travel before it was extremely expensive once again.

With gold, the easiest way to define a criteria over extremely favorable valuation would be to draw a line at a certain forward-return threshold. For example, when our model is projecting 10-year returns greater than 5%/year, let's say.

Recall the following chart:

FIGURE 0.5 PROJECTING FUTURE LONG-TERM RETURNS IN GOLD

Gold moves in *really* long-term cycles. There have only been a few places in history when it was extremely and obviously inexpensive. The first was in the early 1970's as the world was relaxing the gold exchange standard. Gold again became fundamentally cheap relative to its inflationary-trend in 1976-1977. This was after gold had collapsed from a high over nearly $200/oz to a low of $100/oz. Gold was still a somewhat obscure asset class at that point, but by 1980 after it had climbed by a factor of eight, the entire world would be aware of it. (Just in time for a 30 year bear market, accurately predicted by our model!)

The bubble of 1980 was hugely distortive and gold wouldn't get extremely, intrinsically cheap again until the late 1990's.

With these types of very long-term fluctuations, we need to give our signal time to fully play out in accordance with the trend. We might loosely define an "out point" as one in which the 10-year projected rate of return for gold is *negative*. At that point, gold would, theoretically, have approached something of a fair value and no longer command a leveraged or max-weight position.

In our next strategy, we can express this aggressiveness as a 1.5x leveraged position. Again, it may not be practical for all investors to use this exact style of execution, but it will keep the results consistent with the other strategies and highlight the importance of what conditions of extreme undervaluation mean for forward returns.

Trend + Signal Strategy (Leveraged)

Rules & Description:
- When gold's price is above its 12 month moving average, own gold.
- On a monthly close below the 12 month moving average, sell gold and go to cash or Treasuries.
- When the long-term forward returns are projected at 5% or greater, use 1.5x leverage when owning gold rather than a fully long position.

Figure 0.6 Trend + Signal Strategy (Leveraged)

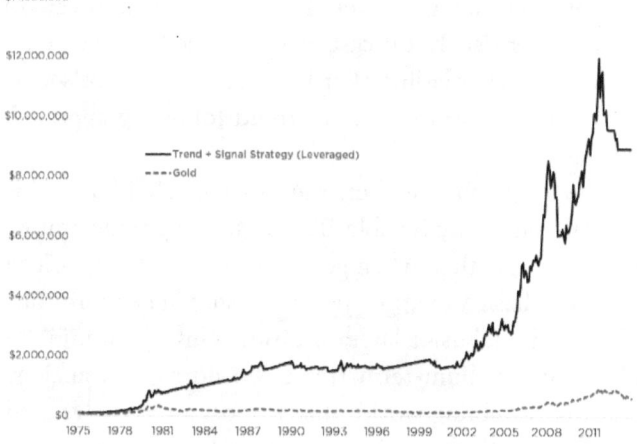

Strategy Performance:
Average Annual Return: 12.22%/yr
Annualized volatility: 19.36%

Buy-and-Hold Performance:
Average Annual Return: 4.81%/yr

Annualized volatility: 19.86%

The returns of this strategy are almost hard to believe. $100,000 invested under this approach in 1975 would have grown to nearly $9 million today versus $624,000 for simply buying and holding gold.

The more interesting thing about this aggressive approach is that the volatility is virtually identical to buying and holding gold. Given the leverage factor involved, it may not necessarily be reasonable to expect that such a strategy would continue to be more volatile than gold in the future. But you can see how important the trend following component is at suppressing long-term volatility. By avoiding most cyclical bear markets in gold, investors not only enjoy a higher overall rate of return, they can do it with lower risk. In the case of a portfolio leveraged 1.5:1, the additional volatility that leverage brings is offset by the amount volatility that our trend following approach reduces.

As mentioned earlier, the exact mechanics of this type of strategy are flexible. The underlying trade philosophy is simply that, when gold is very attractively priced under our basic valuation model, we should be more confident and establish a larger position while continuing to follow the medium-term trend. To borrow an analogy from the gambling world, this approach resembles card counting in Blackjack. When the deck is in our favor – when the long-term expected returns for gold are very high – we bet bigger. When the deck is neutral, we reduce the size of our bets. And when the trend is cold & bearish, we leave the table and go play a different game, or we relax with a drink in the lounge, waiting for the conditions to improve.

Leverage isn't always straightforward to employ. Investors who trade gold via the commodity futures markets will have a very easy time establishing a leveraged position in gold. Leverage is a natural part of the commodities markets and futures contracts. Establishing a leveraged gold position using the physical metal is obviously more challenging. In fact, using the physical metal is highly impractical for any approach that features frequent buys and sells. It should go without saying that none of these strategies should be executed with the physical metal. These should be used only with futures contracts and publicly traded gold ETFs.

✠

It's easy to improve a buy-and-hold approach when it comes to gold. Depending on one's investment objectives, buying and holding gold can be a perfectly appropriate strategy. But investors who are interested in increasing their returns and/or lowering their risk have a broad menu of clearly superior alternatives provided they're willing to take a more active approach.

The set of alternative gold strategies is large, and they can be customized in nearly infinite ways to suit an investor's specific objectives and abilities. The strategies presented here should be used as inspiration, a simple illustration of what else is possible.

In the case of gold, there are myriad ways to approach it that are given hardly any attention at all.

About the Author

Jeffrey Dow Jones has worked for over a decade in the financial industry and has managed investment portfolios of all shapes and sizes. He is the chief strategist and editor for Alpine Advisor, a weekly newsletter and virtual portfolio management service. Jeffrey is also the author of *The Trade of the Decade: A Guide to Investing in the 2010s*.

He lives in Reno, Nevada with his wife, two children, and Westie.

Acknowledgements

This book would not have been possible without the gentle (and increasingly forceful) suggestions of my office mates during that final year of the great gold bull market. Kyle Ferguson, Trinidad Guillen, and poor Kelsey Martin who had to spend her first few months on the job listening to this crazy person rant about gold. Sorry this took so long, guys.

The community at Seeking Alpha also played an instrumental role in the research presented in this book. By making these studies public and opening them up to comment and criticism, I was able to refine and strengthen the underlying theses and incorporate counter-arguments in advance. Ironically, it was the "gold bugs" that helped the most with this. Were it not for their enthusiastic and undying faith in gold, and their willingness to push back against heretics full of criticism, the methods and conclusions presented here would have been both less rigorous and less useful.

www.ingramcontent.com/pod-product-compliance
Lightning Source LLC
Chambersburg PA
CBHW020909180526
45163CB00007B/2683